And We Hav[...]
But As A Merc[...]

The Holy Qur'an, V 107[...]

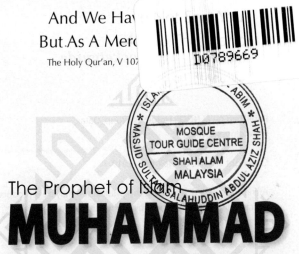

The Prophet of Islam

MUHAMMAD

Biography and Pictorial Guide to the
Moral Basis of the Islamic Civilization

Second Edition

ALNOOR
HOLDINGS

muhammadpocketguide

Published by ALNOOR Holdings Group, Qatar
www.alnoor.com.qa

Printed and bound in Kuwait by Al Qabas Press
Page and Cover design by MANDI Art Design

Feedback and enquiries
info@muhammadpocketguide.com
This book is available on www.amazon.com

ISBN   978-0-9807277-2-2
Second edition, second print, June 2011

My similitude in comparison with the other prophets before me, is that of a man who has built a house completely and excellently except for a place of one brick. When people see the house, they admire its beauty and say: How splendid the house will be if the missing brick is put in its place!
So I am that brick, and I am the last of the Prophets.

Muhammad
(peace be upon him)

(Narrated by Bukhari 4.734, 4.735)

4

Disclaimer & Important Notes

- When Muslims mention Muhammad's name, it is a religious requirement to show respect and say "God's Mercy, Blessing and Peace be upon him". In this book and many other books or publications dealing with Prophet Muhammad, it is abbreviated as (pbuh) "peace be upon him" and in Arabic it is written like this (ﷺ).

  However, since this is a summarized pocket guide where Prophet Muhammad's name is frequently mentioned, it is skipped in some locations so that to save space and not to distract non-Muslim readers. No disrespect is intended.

- This pocket guide refers in several locations to God as "Allah" (personal name of God). This name is not to be used to denote to any other beings. It is a religious requirement that any publication containing the name of God (Allah) must be dealt with respect and must be kept in proper places.

  On the other hand, whenever the word God or Lord is mentioned in this pocket guide, it means Allah (exalted be He).

  Muslims believe in one God (one deity) who created the world, the earth, the heavens, the cosmos and all beings (all nations and all worlds).

According to Islamic belief, God has many attributes or names that describe Him and His deeds such as the Loving (Al-Wadud in Arabic), The Holy (Quddous in Arabic and Qadosh or hakkadosh "The Holy One" in Hebrew), The One (Ahad in Arabic and Echad in Hebrew), The Peace (Salam in Arabic, Shalom in Hebrew). However, His main Name is Allah, exalted be Him.

In Hebrew God is called "Elohim" and in Aramaic God is called "Elah - Alaha". The first chapter in the Holy Qur'an "The Opener" introduces God in the following words: "Praise be to Allah, the Lord of the worlds, the Most Gracious, the Most Merciful".

- The word "Makkah" which is the city where Muhammad (pbuh) was born is spelled as "Mecca" in many text books. Both spellings are used in this book. The city of Makkah is located in the valley of Bakkah which spells "Becca" in the Old Testament. Also, the word "Madina" indicates the city where Muhammad (pbuh) migrated to. In Arabic it is called "Al Madinah Al Munawwarah" which means the enlightened city.

- Information provided in this pocket guide was obtained from authentic sources according to the best knowledge of the author. In case typos or other mistakes were found they would have happened undeliberately. Readers may email their comments to the given contact details in this pocket guide.

ALNOOR
HOLDINGS

The life of Prophet Muhammad (peace be upon him) is still unknown to many people around the world. Despite the fact that many text books have been written about him and his teachings, the media has played a negative role in conveying a distorted picture about him.

Our production of Muhammad pocket guide aims to present the Prophet of Islam objectively to all people worldwide particularly non Muslims and help them obtain a comprehensive, simplified, authentic overview about his character and teachings.

We endeavour to achieve our goals by providing precise and concise information in a simple entertaining pictorial style with the highest international standards.

ALNOOR is an ambitious media group that was established to provide inspirational, value added and responsible textual and visual material. We have positioned ourselves as an all-encompassing global media organisation to effectively penetrate local, regional and international markets with content that is highly appealing and inspirational to the respective audiences. With our international production and animation divisions we focus on producing high quality material including international films, series and documentaries.

Ahmad Al Hashemi
Chairman, ALNOOR Holdings

8

Acknowledgements

Special thanks and gratitude to:

International Support Organization, www.nusrah.org

Al Madinah Research and Studies Center
Madinah - Saudi Arabia

Ministry of Awqaf (Endowments) and Islamic Affairs
Kuwait

Islamic Affairs and Charitable Activities Department
Dubai - UAE

Ahmed Al-Fateh Islamic Centre, Kingdom of Bahrain

Fanar, Islamic Cultural Center – Qatar

Islamic Sciences and Research Academy – Australia

Malaysia Department of Islamic Development – JAKIM

For their kind support and cooperation

I feel honored to have had the time and capabilities to compile this pocket guide about Muhammad (peace be upon him) the man who enlightened the hearts of millions of people around the world and brought them to faith and submission to One God: the Lord of the worlds and all beings.

I spent a very enjoyable time writing and assembling this pocket guide, during which I learnt that a good piece of work needs time and dedication. Facts are precious things and need personal proximity and ambitious effort to record them.

This project (producing the pocket guide) brought me closer to the life, sayings and deeds of Prophet Muhammad (pbuh). I love him and admire him. The more I knew and understood his teachings and way of life, the more motivated I became to present his teachings and sayings to the world in a simple and reliable way.

Muhammad: the man who devoted his life for a noble cause and described himself humbly as the final brick that completed a beautiful building, which represented all prophets and messengers God sent to humanity, to guide them to the truth and protect them from falling astray. This process began from Adam the father of humanity followed by many prophets and messengers (who are recognized by Jews, Christians and Muslims) such as

Noah, Abraham, Isaac, Jacob, Moses, Zachariah, John the Baptist and Jesus (peace and blessings be upon them all).

It is surprising to many readers that Islam has no special rites or rituals related to Muhammad himself. Pilgrimage to the sacred mosque in Mecca, it is mainly Abrahamic. Prophet Abraham had presented one of the greatest example (in the history) for practical submission to God.

After 21 years of hard work and persistence, Prophet Muhammad purified this house from idols and paganism. He restored its original purpose; a house purely for Allah the Lord of the worlds and all beings, where all believers come to worship Him.

Muhammad (pbuh) revered all true prophets and messengers that came before him and acknowledged Jesus with a special honor, when he gave glad tidings to all believers, that Jesus will return one day before the end of life on the earth. He will fight evil, end conflicts and unite all believers in God under his banner. Muhammad (pbuh) asked all Muslims to follow Jesus when he returns and beware of the false messiah.

This pictorial pocket guide is written in a friendly language with an illustrative easy reading style. It is specially written for tourists who visit the Muslim

World or Islamic tourist places and would like to get brief information about the prophet of Islam from Islamic sources. Muhammad, the man who didn't claim to create a new religion but presented himself as the Messenger of God.

The pocket guide is divided into color coded chapters which consist of bold titled paragraphs for easy reading and quick referencing.

I am deeply indebted and profoundly grateful to Mr. Mohammed Dib Abul Razzak, Mrs. Sylvana Mahmic, Mrs. Vicki Snowdon, Dr. Zachariah Mathews, Mr. Peter Gould, Mr. Cyrille Bouzy, Mr. Mehmet Ozalp, Mr. Ali Daher, Ghada Khafagy, Farhat AlKindy and all individuals who contributed with valuable comments to enhance the presentation of the text and contents of the pocket guide.

Also I would like to thank Al-Madinah Research and Studies Center, Madinah – Saudi Arabia for the information, historical data and photos provided.

Dr. Husam Deeb

Table of
Contents

Testimonials

John Adair
Author of "The Leadership of Muhammad". Chair of Leadership Studies United Nations System Staff College in Turin

"In Islamic thought, model leaders were simultaneously both exalted and humble, capable of vision and inspiration, yet at the same time dedicated to the service of their people. As you read these pages, you will, I hope, be able to judge for yourself just how close Muhammad comes to this ideal. My argument in this book is that this ideal -glimpsed more than once in the life of the Prophet Muhammad – accords well with what we know to be the universal truth about the nature and practice of leadership."

William Montgomery Watt
(1909 – 2006) A Scottish historian and Emeritus Professor in Arabic and Islamic Studies at the University of Edinburgh. Author of " Muhammed at Mecca", Oxford, 1953, p. 52

"His readiness to undergo persecutions for his beliefs, the high moral character of the men who believed in him and looked up to him as leader, and the greatness of his ultimate achievement - all argue his fundamental integrity. None of the great figures of history is so poorly appreciated in the West as Muhammad."

Mahatma Gandhi
(1869 - 1948) A political and spiritual leader of the Indian independence movement

"I wanted to know the best one who holds today undisputed sway over the hearts of millions of mankind. I became more than convinced that it was not the sword that won a place for Islam in those days in the scheme of life.

It was the rigid simplicity, the utter self-effacement of Prophet Muhammad, the scrupulous regard for his pledges, his intense devotion to his friends and followers, his intrepidity, his fearlessness, his absolute trust in God and in his own mission. When I closed the second volume (of the book about his life) I was sorry that there was not more for me to read about his great life."

Alphonse de Lamartine
(1790 - 1869) Poet, writer and politician
Histoire De La Turquie, Paris, 1854, Vol. Ii, Pp. 276-277

"Philosopher, orator, apostle, legislator, warrior, conqueror of ideas, restorer of rational dogmas, of a cult without images; the founder of twenty terrestrial empires and of one spiritual empire. That is Muhammad. As regards all standards by which human greatness may be measured, we may well ask, is there any man greater than him?".

William Durant
(1885-1981) Historian, philosopher and writer. Author of "The Story of Civilization", part 4, vol. 4, p. 25

"His name, meaning, "highly praised," lent itself well to certain Biblical passages as predicting his advent. Muhammad was never known to write anything himself; he used an amanuensis. His apparent illiteracy did not prevent him from composing (i.e. conveying the Holy Qur'an which was revealed to him and regarded as) the most famous and eloquent book in the Arabic tongue, and from acquiring such understanding of the management of men as seldom comes to highly educated persons".

Note: *The word amanuensis means someone who writes what is dictated to him. William Durant used the word "composing" which is unacceptable from the Islamic perspective as Muslims believe the Holy Qur'an is a literal Divine revelation from Allah (The Lord of all beings) to Muhammad through Archangel Gabriel.*

Johann Wolfgang Von Goethe
(1749 - 1832) A great European poet. Noten und Abhandlungen zum Weststlichen Dvan, WA I, 7, 32

"He is a prophet and not a poet and therefore his Qur'an is to be seen as Divine Law and not as a book of a human being; made for education or entertainment".

Testimonials

Thomas Carlyle
(1795 - 1881) Historian, philosopher and author of "Heroes and Hero Worship and the Heroic in History"

"How one man single-handedly, could weld warring tribes and wandering Bedouins into a most powerful and civilized nation in less than two decades".

Note: *Thomas Carlyle made an attempt to draw a picture of the development of human intellect by using historical people as coordinates and accorded the Prophet Muhammad a special place in the book under the chapter title "Hero as a Prophet". In his work, Carlyle declared his admiration with a passionate championship of Muhammad as a Hegelian agent of reform.*

Reverend Reginald Bosworth Smith
(Mohammad and Mohammedanism, London, 1874, p. 92)

"Head of the state as well as the Church, he was Caesar and Pope in one; but, he was Pope without the Pope's claims, and Caesar without the legions of Caesar, without a standing army, without a bodyguard, without a palace, without a fixed revenue. If ever any man had the right to say that he ruled by a right Divine, it was Muhammad, for he had all the power without instruments and without its support. He cared not for dressing of power. The simplicity of his private life was in keeping with his public life".

Dr. Salman Bin Fahad Al Audah and a group of scholars

"This is the Messenger of Allah" publication by the "International Support Organization for Prophet Muhammad (pbuh)

"The life of Prophet Muhammad (pbuh) is a great experience of success that all humanity can learn and benefit from, not only Muslims. His social, political, religious and economical success was not because of extraordinary miracles that made his life easy, however, he achieved a genuine success based on hard work, struggle, effort, commitment, competence, love, sincerity and faith. His 23-year-experience was rich in various events and endeavors. He won battles and lost others. He experienced poverty and richness, fear and security. Out of all he successfully conveyed God's Message to mankind.

Muhammad (pbuh) didn't just call for faith in One God but he brought a "Message" for every individual to add value to his/her life and a "Message" for every family to be happy and a "Message" for every society to reinforce brotherhood and a "Message" for every nation to emphasize solidarity and development and a "Message" for humanity to strengthen knowledge, love and cooperation."

This is the word Muhammad in Arabic written in a formative style. It looks like the upper part of a mosque with a dome in the middle. Please note the dome is the letter "h" in the word "Muhammad". The lower part of the mosque is formed from the sentence "rasoolu-Allah" which means the "Messenger of God".

The hexagon is formed from the Arabic word "Muhammad" being written in a different style of Arabic calligraphy and repeated 6 times.

Courtesy of Plastic Artist Mr. Farid Al-Ali

In Arabic, the word " Muhammad" means the person who is highly, frequently and repeatedly praised for his good deeds. Therefore, he is a praiseworthy person.

His Character

Muhammad Attributes Portrait : Documented character and attributes as seen by his companions.
Courtesy of calligrapher Abdul Ilah Abu Jaish

Muhammad's Character and Attributes

His Character

What did he look like?

Muhammad (peace be upon him) was a white man with a rosy tinge. He was of a height a little above the average. He was well built with broad shoulders. His belly never protruded out of his chest profile. He used to walk briskly and firmly, lifting each foot off the ground.

Muhammad's companions described him as a handsome person with prominent forehead, high tipped nose, long eyelashes, large black eyes with well set teeth and a pleasant smile. He had slightly curly hair and a thick beard.

His companions indicated that he had a friendly bright face that looked like a full moon. He did not laugh loudly; his laugh was mostly a smile that would show his teeth a bit like hailstones. His cheerfulness and open personality were felt by all people.

His nature

Muhammad (peace be upon him) was unfailingly cheerful, easy going by nature, and mild mannered. He was not a clamorous loud mouth, nor a repeater of obscenities. He was not a fault finder, nor did he overly praise the others.

The way he spoke

Muhammad (peace be upon him) did not speak unnecessarily and what he said was always to the point and without any padding. His sayings were precise and concise having complete meaning in few words. He spoke with excellence, and there was no excess in it and no abnormal brevity.

When he emphasized a point, he used to repeat it thrice with a gesture. He spoke of nothing unless he hoped a reward from God for it. He told his companions:

"I am a guarantor for a house in the heart of the Paradise for those who quit arguing even if they were right and I am a guarantor for a house in the middle of the Paradise for those who quit lying even if they were kidding and I am a guarantor for a house in the highest part in the Paradise for those who behave with good manners." (Sahih Abu Dawood)

His passions

He kept his feelings under firm control. When annoyed, he would turn aside or keep silent. When someone commits an act that violates God's Law, he used to show serious anger and firm stand. No one would stand against his anger when matters of the Lord's truth were opposed, until he had triumph, but he would never get angry for his own sake.

How did he deal with people?

Muhammad (peace be upon him) was always the first to greet the others and would not withdraw his hand from a hand shaker till the other man withdrew his.

Whoever saw him unexpectedly would admire and revere him. And whoever socialized or associated with him familiarly, loved him. He was gentle by nature. He was neither coarse nor disdainful of anyone.

When he looked at the others, he looked at them in full face. If someone called him he didn't turn his face only, but gave attention with his whole body.

When he would go to visit a group, he would sit in the nearest available spot. He ordered his companions to follow his practice. He would give those seated near him his full share of attention in such a way that no one would think others had been given precedence over him. He didn't reserve fixed places among the people to be seated. He was fair with his companions and all people. They were distinguished only by virtue and devotion to God.

His style of living

Everything he did was in moderation, without excess or contrariness. He never criticized the food or drink that was prepared for him, nor did he overly praise it.

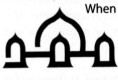

When at home, he would divide his time into three parts, one for God, one for his family, and one for himself. He always joined in household work and would at times mend his clothes, repair his shoes and sweep the floor. He used to dress well and smell good.

(Sahih Bukhari, Chapter: Kitabul Adab)

After dawn prayers, he would remain sitting in the mosque reciting the Holy Qur'an and praises of Allah, till the sun rose. After midnight, he used to get up for the (Tahajjud) prayers which he never missed even once in his life (Bukhari, Sahih Bukhari).

He had declared unlawful for himself and his family anything given by the people by way of zakat or sadaqa (types of charity). He was so particular about it, that he would not appoint any member of his family as a zakat collector.

His house was but a hut with walls of unbaked clay and a thatched roof of palm leaves covered by camel skin.

Muhammad (pbuh) said : "What have I to do with worldly things. My connection with the world is like that of a traveler resting for a while underneath the shade of a tree and then moving on."

When he died, he did not leave a cent or any property except his white mule and a piece of land which he had dedicated for the good of the community (Sahih Bukhari).

His Character

Prophet Muhammad's Mosque as described and imagined

Prophet Muhammad's house as described and imagined

Biography

Personal Details

Name	**Muhammad**
Father's Name	Abdullah, son of Abdul-Muttalib (ancestry reaches back to the Prophet Ishmael son of Prophet Abraham)
Surname	He was from Bani-Hashim family (Bani-Hashim was from Quraysh, a tribe that was highly ranked in Arabia)
Date of Birth	22nd April, 570 CE [1]
Place of Birth	City of Mecca – Arabian Peninsula (currently in Saudi Arabia)
Date of Death	6th June, 632 CE. (he was 63 years old when he passed away)
Death & Burial Place	City of Madinah (approximately 450 km north of Mecca)

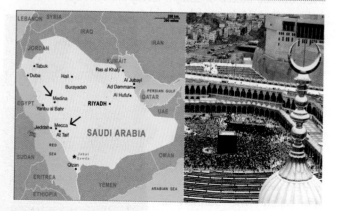

Childhood & Adolescence

Birth - 2 years old	Muhammad had no brothers or sisters. His father passed away before he was born. His mother sent him out of Mecca to be breastfed by a wet nurse called Halima (this was an old Arab custom).
2-6 years old	He lived with his mother Amina until she passed away in the year 576 CE.
6-8 years old	He lived with his grandfather Abdul-Muttalib until he passed away.
8-25 years old	He lived with his paternal uncle (Abu-Talib) who had 10 children.

Education

Muhammad was illiterate: He could not read or write. He never lived outside Mecca or sought foreign knowledge. Muslims believe that Muhammad (pbuh) conveyed the "Holy Qur'an" as the Message of God and His Book to all people. He conveyed it letter by letter and word by word without rephrasing any part of it with his own words.

Muhammad's sayings and teachings were not mixed with the Holy Qur'an: They were collected in books which are called "The Sunnah of the Prophet" which means his teachings, way of life and explanation of the Book (The Holy Qur'an).

Working Life

Childhood – mid twenties	He worked as a shepherd for some time (looking after sheep and goats for others). In addition, he worked in trading with his uncle Abu-Talib. According to authentic narrations, Muhammad was 12 years old when he, for the first time, joined his uncle Abu-Talib in a trading trip to Syria.
Mid twenties - 40 years old	He worked as a merchant or a trader for a wealthy woman called Khadijah who had a general trading business (they used to buy commodities from one area and sell them in another). Muhammad was known in his community as a successful and honest tradesman. He was famous for his fidelity, integrity and trustworthiness. It was not long before he earned the title of **"As-Sadiqul Ameen"** which means "the truthful and the trustworthy".
40-63 years old	When he was 40 years old (year 610 CE) Muhammad received the divine revelation and dedicated his life to conveying God's Message to all people. He taught people the oneness of God and conveyed God's Book (The Qur'an) which calls for social justice, peace, harmony and wellbeing.

Marital Status

Married to one wife for 25 years: Muhammad married Khadijah, the daughter of Khuwaylid, who came from a noble family called Asad.[2]

She was a respected woman in her community and she was a widow. Muhammad worked for her for two years before she proposed marriage to him through a third party. She found him a very loyal, transparent and ethical person.

Successful marriage: Although Khadijah was 15 years older than Muhammad, both of them came from a similar social class in the community.

The age difference was no obstacle to the establishment of a successful marriage which lasted for 25 years until Khadijah died in the year 619 CE at the age of 65.

Muhammad remarried after Khadijah passed away.

A father of 6 children and a family man:

Muhammad & Khadijah lived in harmony and peace; they had four daughters (Zaynab, Ruqayya, Um Kulthoum & Fatima) and two sons (Al-Qassim who died when he was 3 years old and Abdullah who died

> **Muhammad loved Khadijah and was loyal to her and his children**
>
> On several occasions he described her as the best woman of her time alike to Mary the mother of Jesus who was the best woman of her time.
>
> *(Narrated by Bukhari)*

at the age of 4). Muhammad used to spend time with his family, help his wife in house matters, sew his own clothes and look after his children.

Photo taken from Baqee Cemetery which is next to Prophet Muhammad Mosque in Madinah. Some of Muhammad's companions, relatives, wives and children were buried in this cemetery

Al-Ma'ala cemetery in Mecca where Khadijah was buried

Mission Accomplished in 23 Years

610 CE

Divine revelation commenced:
Muhammad (pbuh) received the Message of God [3]. He was appointed as the Messenger of God to convey God's Words to humanity. A mission that required strong belief, dedication, commitment and honesty.

610- 612 CE

Core Muslims formed:
Muhammad invited his friends, his inner circle and selected good quality people, to accept Islam. In the first three years after prophecy, around 130 people accepted Islam and became a strong nucleus that was able to spread Islam publicly. These core Muslims were a mix of rich and poor people.

613- 615 CE

Muhammad's public invitation resisted:
Muhammad and his followers started to talk to people openly about Islam. Although Muhammad was known as a trustworthy and

an honest man, Meccan leaders did not accept his invitation to embrace Islam and resisted him. They described him as a poet, a magician and a crazy man.

Muhammad tempted and threatened: Meccan leaders tried to dissuade Muhammad from calling people to Islam by tempting and threatening him. At the same time they tried to prevent people from listening to him. They showed increased hostility towards new Muslims. They persecuted and tortured the poor and weak Muslims.

Muhammad supported his followers and sent some of them to Abyssinia: Muhammad was very close to his followers. He used to meet them at Al-Arqam House which was like a small college. He taught them values and morals and instilled feelings of responsibility and commitment.

Muhammad saw the suffering and tribulation some of his followers endured and advised them to seek refuge in Abyssinia, describing it as a land of virtue ruled by a fair Christian king, under whom no one was treated unjustly.

Two influencial men embraced Islam: Two strong and well respected Meccan men accepted Islam, Omar Bin Al-Khattab and Hamza Bin Abdul-Muttalib (Muhammad's uncle). That was an important turning point for Muslims. Hamza became a strong supporter and protector for Muhammad until he (Hamza) died in the battle of Uhud (625 CE). Three years after the passing away of Prophet Muhammad (pbuh), Omar became the second caliph and ruled the Islamic state for 11 years.

616- 618 CE

Muhammad boycotted: Meccan leaders boycotted Muhammad and his followers and imposed a social and economical blockade on them which lasted for 3 years. During this time, Muhammad and his followers suffered great tribulation. This period was a tough test for their patience, belief and commitment to the truth.

619- 620 CE

A Sorrowful year: Meccan chiefs cancelled the social and economical blockade as they found it not useful. In the same year, Muhammad's wife Khadijah and his uncle Abu-Talib passed away.

Muhammad (pbuh) lost hope in Mecca and decided to convey the Message of God and seek support outside Mecca. He went to the city of Ta'if but was met with hostility[4]. In addition, he spoke to more than 20 Arab tribes about Islam but he didn't receive any positive response.

620- 622 CE

A glimpse of hope: Muhammad met six people from Yathrib (a city located 450 km north of Mecca) during the pilgrimage time and talked to them about Islam. They believed Muhammad (pbuh) and returned to their city with intentions to invite more people from their own tribe and other tribes in Yathrib. They agreed to return to Mecca the next year at the time of pilgrimage to meet again with Muhammad "the Prophet and the Messenger of God".

New Muslims pledged allegiance to Muhammad:

The same group returned the following year (621 CE) with six more people [5]. They pledged their allegiance to Muhammad (pbuh) (accepting him as the Messenger of God) and promising him:

Aqaba or Al-Bay'aa "Pledge" Mosque

(1) not to worship anyone except (Allah) The One God, (2) not to steal, (3) not to commit adultery, (4) not to kill, (5) not to slander neighbours and (6) not to disobey the Messenger of God.

The group went back to Yathrib and invited their tribal leaders and their people to accept Islam. They returned again in the following year (622 CE) at the time of pilgrimage with more than 70 men and two women. A similar pledge of allegiance was given again to Prophet Muhammad (pbuh).

A new Muslim community formed 450 km north of Mecca: The leaders of the two main tribes in Yathrib (Aws & Khazraj) embraced Islam and subsequently their people became Muslims. Muhammad the Prophet (pbuh) was invited to come to Yathrib and become its ruler and leader.

622 CE
Chiefs of Mecca plotted to kill Muhammad; migration to Yathrib commenced: Things were becoming worse in Mecca. Muhammad asked Meccan Muslims[6] to migrate to Yathrib. Following their migration, Muhammad (pbuh) migrated to Yathrib in September 622 CE. His migration represents the most important turning point in the Islamic history. From Yathrib, Islam blossomed, an Islamic state was established and a just social order was born.

623-624 CE
Muhammad chosen the ruler of Yathrib:
The people of Yathrib were a mix of Arabs and Jews. Although there were two main Arab tribes and three smaller Jewish tribes, the Arab community was larger than the Jewish one and had the ruling power. Muhammad, "The Prophet of God" was chosen as the ruler of Yathrib willingly and peacefully with the agreement of the majority of people.

Muhammad changed the name of the multicultural society: "Madinah" was the new name Muhammad (pbuh) gave to the city of Yathrib.

After the migration of the Meccan Muslims, Yathrib no longer belonged to a certain group of Arabs, instead, it became the homeland of believers who accepted Islam.

Since there were Jewish tribes in Yathrib and other Arab people who didn't embrace Islam, Muhammad (pbuh) did not call it the city of Islam. Instead, it was named "Al-Madinah" which means "The City", in which all inhabitants had similar citizenship rights.

Muhammad called for peace and unity in Madinah:
In his first public address to the people of Madinah, Muhammad delivered a very concise speech which promoted harmony and social cohesion.

He said: "O People, seek and spread peace and offer food to each other, look after your kinship and pray to God at night while others are sleeping so you gain God's pleasure and enter His paradise".

Muhammad linked these acts to God's pleasure in order to motivate people to love each other and live in peace and harmony in a multicultural society.

623-624 CE

Muhammad formed the first constitution and charter of human rights and liberties: Most of the Jews hoped that the last Prophet would come from a Jewish background. Although the majority of Jews did not accept Muhammad as a Messenger of God, Muhammad (as the ruler of the state) formed the first "Constitution and Charter of Human Rights and Liberties" to which all Arab and Jewish tribes agreed upon and signed.

The constitution guaranteed the freedom of conscience and worship for Muslims and Jews as well as Arabs who did not accept Islam.

In addition, the constitution protected the safety and security of all citizens in Madinah and required all parties who signed the covenant for the constitution to be part of the national defence should Madinah be attacked by enemies. The constitution stated justice, human rights, liberties and prohibition of crime and immoral practices.

624 CE

The unavoidable battle of Badr: When Muslims migrated from Mecca to Madinah, many of them were forced to abandon their homes and their properties were confiscated.

Location of Badr

The chiefs of Mecca used the confiscated money in trade and business. Muslims knew about a trade caravan belonging to the Meccan chiefs, led by their enemy Abu-Sufyan which would pass through a trade route close to Madinah.

Muhammad (pbuh) called upon Muslims to take the caravan in return for their wealth that was confiscated in Mecca. A force of only 313 Muslims took up the mission. The Meccan intelligence advised Abu-Sufyan to change the route of the trade caravan. In addition, Mecca sent an army of 950 soldiers to fight the Muslim force which was not prepared for war and was far less equipped than the Meccan army.

It was astonishing and beyond expectation that Muslims won their first battle against the Meccan chiefs. Many Meccan chiefs and important figures were killed in this battle.

625 CE

Meccan chiefs attacked Muhammad and his followers in the battle of Uhud: In retaliation for their loss in the battle of Badr and their fear of losing their leading role in Arabia, Meccan chiefs with some Arab allies, sent an army of 3000 soldiers to attack Muslims at the mount of Uhud north of Madinah.

Location of Uhud - Madinah - Saudi Arabia

The Muslims lost this battle and Muhammad (Pbuh) was wounded but saved. In the battle of Uhud some of Muhammad's companions were killed including his beloved uncle Hamza.

Martyrs of Uhud Battle, Uhud cemetery - Madinah - Saudi Arabia

626 CE

Meccans and other tribes attacked Muhammad and his followers in the battle of trench: This battle is also called the "Battle of Confederates". Since Muhammad was not killed in the previous battle, Meccan chiefs and some Arab & Jewish tribes called for a united effort and a comprehensive assault to kill Muhammad and destroy the Muslim community.

10,000 soldiers marched towards Madinah. After consulting his companions, Muhammad (pbuh) decided to adopt the proposal of a Persian Muslim named Salman to dig a trench on the northern access of Madinah (5.5 km long X 4.6m wide).

Muslims were in their most awkward situation and tried their best including psychological warfare, to defend themselves. After a month-long siege the meccan army and its allies became impatient and strong storms and wind blew which forced the confederates to pack up their tents and withdraw.

627 CE

Treaty of Hudaybiya, a truce for 10 years: One year after the battle of trench, Muhammad (pbuh) took a peaceful initiative to perform Umrah (visit the Ka'bah House of God in Mecca and perform other religious rites) . Visiting Mecca for the purpose of worship was a religious right that Mecca undertook to give to all people in Arabia.

10-Year Truce

It was a great surprise for Meccan chiefs to see Muhammad approaching Mecca with 1400 civilians coming from Madinah.

After several negotiations, a truce was made between the Meccan chiefs and Muhammad (pbuh) for 10 years during which time Muhammad and his companions returned to their homes with a condition to come again to visit Mecca in the following year (628 CE). The truce had many other terms with which the Muslims were disappointed because they weighed heavily on the Meccan side.

628- 629 CE
During the truce, Muhammad conveyed God's Message inside & outside Arabia: The truce was a golden chance for Muhammad (pbuh) to convey the Message of God and freely talk to people about Islam without being stopped or intercepted by other forces.

Muhammad (pbuh) sent delegations to other Arab tribes in Arabia and wrote letters to the rulers and kings of

neighbouring countries and superpowers such as Persia, Byzantine and Egypt inviting them to accept Islam as "the Message of God". Muslims increased in numbers as people found the truth in Islam.

630 CE

Peaceful take-over of Mecca: Within less than 2 years, the truce was broken from the Meccan side when their allies killed 20 Muslims.

In response to this shocking act, Muhammad (pbuh) marched with 10,000 Muslims to conquer Mecca but asked his soldiers not to fight any one unless they were fought.[7]

The Meccan chiefs were embarrassed and were not prepared to fight the Muslims. When the Muslim army arrived in Mecca, Muhammad (pbuh) addressed the whole people of Mecca confirming the oneness of God, referring victory to Him and reminding people that all of them descended from Adam and Adam was created from dust of the ground.

Then he asked the people of Mecca "What do you expect me to do with you?. They replied: "We hope for the best. After all, you have been a gracious brother and a courteous cousin".

Exemplar forgiveness: Despite the hardship caused by the Meccan people during the last 21 years, Muhammad (pbuh) behaved with high moralities. He replied: "Have no fear today. Depart then (to your homes), you are free". Muhammad's address was very influential and many people came to him to make a pledge and embrace Islam.

630 - 631 CE
Arab tribes embraced Islam: After the peaceful takeover of Mecca, delegations from all over Arabia came to learn about Islam. Except the Hawazen tribe who fought the Muslims and eventually lost the battle of Hunayn, most Arab tribes embraced Islam. Muhammad (pbuh) sent many of his companions to various provinces in Arabia to teach people Islam "The Message of God".

At the same event, Muhammad(pbuh) knocked down all idols around and on the Ka'bah (The House of God) which was erected by Prophet Abraham (pbuh) to glorify one God (The Creator of the universe and all beings).

632 CE

Muhammad's farewell address: Muhammad's mission was accomplished and his life was nearing to an end. In the year 632 CE Muhammad (pbuh) performed pilgrimage and gave his final sermon to more than 100,000 people.

His sermon reminded people about the basic elements of faith, belief in One God, sanctity of life, wealth & property, equality of all races, rules of justice, women's rights and obligations, exploitation and monopoly, morality and the rights of others.

632 CE

The passing away of Muhammad:

Prophet Muhammad (pbuh) passed away in his home in Madinah in the year 632 CE leaving only few possessions. He did not leave any money or wealth but a legacy of faith, that is still illuminating with God's light, the hearts of millions of people around the globe.

To err is human, to forgive is Divine - Alexander Pope

Mountains in Makkah - Saudi Arabia

Panoramic view for the mount of Light where cave Hira exists - Makkah

Aerial view of the sacred mosque, Makkah - Saudi Arabia

جبل ثور

Thawr Cave, the cave Muhammad (pbuh) and his companion Abu Baker rested in for three nights in the beginning of his trip (migration to Madinah)

According to authentic narrations, Muhammad (pbuh) and his companion Abu Bakr rested near a large rock on the migration way from Mecca to Madinah –The above rock was found on the same way of migration trip and it is believed to be the same rock

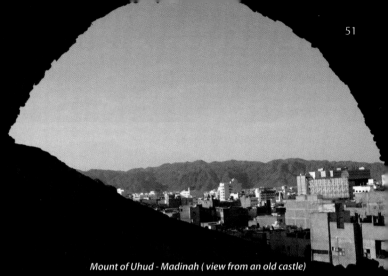

Mount of Uhud - Madinah (view from an old castle)

Palm trees in Madinah

Aerial view of Badr town

The area where Quraish Army camped

Location of Battle of Badr, the area where Muhammad (pbuh) and his companions camped

Location of Battle of Badr

Panoramic view, Uhud Mountain

Location of Uhud battle. The photo shows the archery mount and the cemetery of Martyrs. More than seventy of Muhammad's companions and his beloved uncle Hamza are buried there.

Trench Battle

Mount of Uhud

Waqem Harra (Volcanic Area)

Location of the trench

Silaa Mount

M a d i n a h   C i t y

Wabra Harra (Volcanic Area)

Qubaa' Mosque; the first mosque in Islam,
8 km south of the Nabawi mosque – Madinah - KSA

Qubaa' Mosque – Madinah - KSA

An imaginery view of Madinah City showing Prophet Muhammad's (Pbuh) mosque (Nabawi Mosque) surrounded by houses and palm trees. (Courtesy of : Madinah Research and Studies Center, Saudi Arabia)

An imaginery view of the Prophet Muhammad's (Pbuh) mosque (Nabawi Mosque) which was built after his arrival to Madinah. His house was built at the southern corner of the mosque.

58

Late King Fahad Bin Abdul Aziz Al Saud inaugurating the latest extension of the Nabawi mosque – 1986 Madinah – Saudi Arabia

Inside the latest extension of the Nabawi Mosque – Madinah – Saudi Arabia

Nabawi mosque (Prophet Muhammad (pbuh) Mosque) – Madinah – Saudi Arabia

Sunset view of Nabawi mosque

Inside and outside of Nabawi Mosque

61

Rawda Area where Prophet Muhammad (pbuh) used to give the speech of Friday cermon

The tomb of Prophet Muhammad (pbuh)

The tomb of Prophet Muhammad (pbuh) at the Nabawi Mosque in Madinah. Next to it are the tombs of the first Caliph (successor) and ruler of the Islamic state Abu Bakir Al Siddiq and the second Caliph Omar Bin Al-Khattab.

Among the known prophets of God, Muhammad (pbuh) is the only prophet that his burial place is precisely identified and his followers are certain about the exact location of his tomb.

Muhammad (pbuh) was buried at his house which is attached to his mosque "Al Nabawi Mosque" in Madinah.

This photo shows the side of the mosque building where people can enter to see the tomb of Prophet Muhammad (pbuh) and his house which is currently caged.

Al-Masjid Al-Nabawi Al-Sharif
(Nabawi Mosque). Courtesy of Photographer Noushad Ali

Aerial view of Makkah, Saudi Arabia
showing the Sacred Mosque (Al-Masjid Al-Haram)

FOOTNOTES

1 According to some narrations and calculations Muhammad (pbuh) was born in the year 571 CE.

2 Some narrations state that the marriage of Muhammad (pbuh) and Khadijah lasted for 24 years and several months.

3 There is one and only one Qur'an which is revealed to Muhammad (pbuh) in original Arabic. However, there are many translations for the meanings of the verses in the Holy Qur'an to different languages such as English, French, Chinese, etc. The quoted verses in this pocket guide from the Holy Qur'an are presented in simple English based on the English translation mentioned in the cited references.

4 Muhammad (pbuh) was attacked in Tai'f and experienced the worst treatment there. When he left Taif he was very disappointed. According to some narrations, he called God with a wonderful supplication (see next page).

5 Aqaba or Al-Bay'aa "Pledge" Mosque: established by the Abbasside Caliph Abu Jaafar Al Manssour on the same place that is believed the new Muslims from Madinah pledged commitment to Prophet Muhammad (pbuh) as they embraced Islam.

6 A small Muslim community stayed in Mecca and were not able to migrate to Yathrib (Madinah).

7 The Islamic calendar starts from the date Muhammad (pbuh) migrated from Mecca to Madinah (13th Sep 622 CE approx. The peaceful taking over of Mecca was on the 8th Jan 630 CE approx).

Muhammad's Supplication To God

O my Lord, it is to You that I bring my weakness,
helplessness & humiliation.

O The Most Merciful of the merciful ones,
You are the Sustainer of those who are deemed weak
and You are my Sustainer.

On whom (but You) shall I rely? On somebody distant
who regards me with displeasure or on a foe (enemy) to
whom I have surrendered.

So long as You are not displeased with me, then I
have no cause for sadness.

I take refuge in your light by which the darkness is
illuminated and in which both this world and the next
are set aright.

The well-being which You bestow upon me is too
all-encompassing for You to pour out Your anger or
displeasure upon me.

To You I shall continue to turn until I have won Your
favour.

Prophecy

محمّد

Mount of Noor / Hira Cave
Makkah - Saudi Arabia

Muhammad & Prophecy

Muhammad didn't know that he would be a Prophet: He led an ethical and ordinary life. He was known for his fidelity, integrity and trustworthiness. He never worshipped idols when idol worship was rife in a polytheistic society.

He always believed that the whole universe must have been created and controlled by one God. He used to worship God by retreating to a cave (634m above sea level) in a mount 4 km east of Mecca (Makkah).

The cave is known as cave Hira in the mount of Hira or Noor (i.e. light); this is because Muhammad received revelation from God when he was meditating in this cave.

Hira Cave

It wasn't illusion and it wasn't a dream: When Muhammad reached forty years old, he used to meditate frequently in Cave Hira. At the month of Ramadan (the ninth month of the lunar year, 610 CE approx), Archangel Gabriel appeared to him for the first time while he was in the cave and asked him to "Read". Muhammad was frightened.

Read !

As he was illiterate, he could not read and did not know what to read. Archangel Gabriel repeated his word "read" again and again then he recited the following verses from God:

> "Read in the Name of your Lord Who created (every thing), He created man from a clot (clinging to the wall of the womb)...Read ! and your Lord is the All-Munificent.. Who has taught man by the pen...He taught man what he didn't know!"
>
> The Holy Qur'an, V 1-5, Ch 96

Archangel Gabriel disappeared after this short meeting.

Muhammad was terrified: He was extremely scared. He ran back to his home. He was trembling. He told his wife Khadijah what happened to him and asked her to cover him.

She told him that God would not let him down or allow devils to touch him as he kept good relations with his relatives, helped the poor people and liked doing charity.

A Divine revelation or satanic whispers? Muhammad was afraid that he was possessed by evil. He went with his wife Khadijah to tell the whole story to Waraqa Bin Nawfal (a relative of Khadijah) who was a religious Christian person and knowledgeable in the Bible. Waraqa predicted that Muhammad would be a Prophet and assured him that what he experienced was a Divine revelation similar to what Moses the Prophet of Jews received. Waraqa wished to support Muhammad but he was very old at that time. He told Muhammad that he would be driven out of Makkah by his own people and would be treated with hostility by some people.

You are God's Messenger: Muhammad needed a few days to settle down and didn't return to the mount. After sometime Archangel Gabriel came back to him and informed him that he would be a messenger of God, Allah The Lord of all beings. He recited the following verse from Allah (exalted be Him):

> *"O you cloaked (enveloped in your garments); Arise and warn; and glorify your Lord; and purify your clothing; and keep away from bad deeds and don't consider your fulfilment of these orders as a favour to God or people; and be patient for the sake of your Lord"*
> The Holy Qur'an, V 1-7, Ch 74

Gabriel continued to see Muhammad (pbuh) over a period of 23 years during which the Holy Qur'an (God's Words) was revealed to Muhammad by Gabriel in order to convey it to all mankind.

Muhammad conveyed Gods' Commandments to his people : Muhammad acted according to the revelation he received in year 610 CE. He invited his people and the whole Arabia to believe in one God (Allah) and obey His Commandments as they are set for the wellbeing of the whole humanity.

What is the "Message" about? The Message of Islam is based on "Aqidah" i.e. creed (as a statement of faith and belief in One God the creator of all beings) and "Shariah" i.e. God's Law; the system and regulations that govern people's day to day transactions, activities and practices.

Shariah is divided into three main branches: (1) Worship: religious practices and deeds such as daily prayers, fasting, supplications, giving Zakat (alms), etc. (2)  Morals: good behaviors, etiquettes and values such as honesty, sincerity, fidelity, love, cooperation, etc. (3) Life transactions and dealings: (Islamic civil law) rules of justice, people's rights, commerce, etc).

Note: After receiving divine revelation, Muhammad focused on teaching people monotheism (Aqidah) for thirteen years. After migration to Madinah, there was more focus on explaining and implementing Shariah.

God's Commandments

"Say (O Muhammad):
Come, I will recite what your Lord
prohibited you from,
(1) Don't join any partners as equal with
Him; (2) And be good to your parents; (3)
And don't kill your children on a plea of
want, We provide sustenance for you and for
them; (4) And don't approach or get close to
doing shameful deeds openly or secretly (e.g.
adultery and deeds of corruption);

(5) And don't kill any soul which God made
sacred except by way of justice and law. This
is what He commands you, thus you may
learn wisdom;
(6) And don't touch the orphans' wealth or
property, except to improve it, until he or she
reaches maturity;

(7, 8) And give measure and weight with
(full) justice (when buying & selling and
when doing financial & non financial
transactions), We place no burdens on any
one but that which he or she can bear; (9) And
whenever you speak (or bear witness) speak
justly even if near relative is concerned; (10)
And fulfil the Covenant of God. This is what
He commands you that you may remember "

The Holy Qur'an V 151, 152 , Ch 6

A practical introduction of Muhammad's teachings in Abyssinia: Ja'far bin Abi-Talib was among eighty Muslims who fled for protection in the land of Abyssinia (currently Ethiopia in Africa). Speaking to the King of Abyssinia on behalf of the Muslims who sought asylum there, Ja'far said:

"O King, we were once people living in ignorance (lack of knowledge and unawareness), worshiping idols, eating carrion, committing acts of abomination, neglecting our kith & kin, treating our neighbours badly and allowing the strong among us to oppress the weak. This is how we lived until God sent us a messenger from among ourselves, a man whose family origin, honesty, integrity and chastity were well known to us.

He called upon us to worship God alone and leave away the stones and idols which we worshipped as our forefathers had done. He instructed us to be truthful in our words, to fulfil our promises and to respect our obligations to our blood relations and he forbade us from committing abominations.

So we trusted & believed him and followed the message he received from God. However, our people denounced us, tortured us and did everything in their capacity to turn us away from our religion. When they continued to oppress us, we came to your land choosing you above all others in order to get protection and be treated with impartiality."

A Christian King acknowledged Muhammad's religion:
After Ja'far delivered his talk, the King of Abyssinia (who was a religious and God fearing person) asked Ja'far to recite some of the "Book" revealed to Muhammad. Ja'far recited a portion from the chapter "Mary"[1] in the Holy Qur'an until the King wept and his beard was moist with tears.

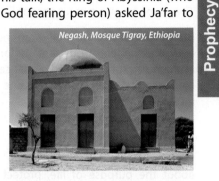

Negash, Mosque Tigray, Ethiopia

The King then said:

"The message brought by Muhammad and that which was brought by Jesus are from a single source".

One God..One Message

The prophets and messengers of God in the Holy Qur'an:

Islam acknowledges all prophets and messengers God sent before Muhammad (pbuh) for the guidance of humanity. They confirmed one message "monotheism" which is the belief in God's existance and oneness.

God sent them to educate people about the purpose of life, protect them from falling astray and teach them good morals.

The Holy Qur'an mentioned 25 prophets and messengers by name and focused on the stories of some of them. For example, in the Holy Qur'an Adam was mentioned 25 times, Noah was mentioned 43 times, Abraham was mentioned 69 times, Moses was mentioned 136 times and Jesus was mentioned 25 times.

> Muhammad (pbuh) said: "My similitude in comparison with the other prophets before me, is that of a man who has built a house completely and excellently except for a place of one brick. When people see the house, they admire its beauty and say: how splendid the house will be if the missing brick is put in its place. So I am that brick, and I am the last of the Prophets ". (Narrated by Bukhari 4.734, 4.735)

Prophecy

Verily We sent messengers before you, among them those of whom We have told you (their story), and some of whom We have not told you (their story); and it was not given to any messenger that he should bring a sign (miracle) except by God's leave (permission)

The Holy Qur'an, V 78, Ch 40

Say : We have believed in Allah and that which is revealed unto us and that which was revealed unto Abraham, and Ishmael, and Isaac, and Jacob and the tribes, and that which Moses and Jesus received, and that which the Prophets received from their Lord. We make no distinction between any of them, and unto Him we have surrendered.

The Holy Qur'an, V 136, Ch 2

Torah, Gospel and Qur'an are God's revelations to mankind: Believing in God's revealed Books before the Holy Qur'an is an essential pillar of the Islamic faith. Muslims believe that the Holy Qur'an does not contradict previous revelations but it does point out and correct deviations from truth that happened through the history.

We did reveal the Torah, where in it there is guidance and a light. The Holy Qur'an, V 44, Ch 5

And We sent following in their footsteps, Jesus, the son of Mary confirming that which came before him in the Torah, and We gave him the Gospel in which was guidance and light and confirming that which preceded it of the Torah as guidance and instructions for the righteous.

The Holy Qur'an, V 46, Ch 5

And unto you (Muhammad) We revealed the Book (The Holy Qur'an) with the truth, confirming whatever Scripture was before it, and a watcher (criterion) over it.

The Holy Qur'an, V 48, Ch 5

Those whom God bestowed favor among the Prophets, of the descendents of Adam and of those whom We carried (in the ship) with Noah, and of the seed of Abraham and Israel, and from among those whom We guided and chose. When the revelations of (The Lord) The Beneficent were recited unto them, they fell in prostration, adoring and weeping.

The Holy Qur'an, V 58, Ch 19

Table 1: The life of main prophets

Prophet	Muhammad	Jesus	Moses	Abraham
Approx. Period	570 - 632 CE	1-33 CE	around 1400 BC	around 1700 BC
Approx. Age	63	33	120	175

Muhammad and Abraham:

Abraham is considered as the father of prophets in the Jewish, Christian and Islamic religions because most of the known prophets were from his offspring. Muslims believe that prophet Muhammad is his descendent through his first son Ishmael who was also the father of many Arab tribes. On the other hand, the nation of Israel and many prophets such as Jacob, Joseph, Aaron and Moses have descended from his second son Isaac.

Abraham dedicated his life and struggled to teach people monotheism. The Holy Qur'an frequently mentioned Abraham and indicated that after he put an effort in searching for the truth and recognized the oneness of God "The One Deity", Abraham practically proved his sincerity, honesty, thankfulness and obedience to God. He presented one of the greatest and most memorable examples in the history for full submission to One God even in the most difficult situations.

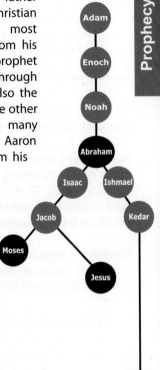

Who is better in religion than the one who submits him / herself to Allah (surrender his/her purpose to God) while being a doer of good and follows the religion of Abraham (tradition inclining towards truth, the upright? And Allah chose Abraham as an intimate friend.

The Holy Qur'an, V 125, Ch 4

He was a man of truth who showed an exemplar obedience to God, therefore, according to the Holy Qur'an, God chose Abraham as a friend and as one of the elite in the World and among the righteous in the

One God

Hereafter (V125, Ch 4, V130, Ch 2). He guided him to the right religion and made him an "Imam" i.e. a leader for people (V124, Ch 2) and described him as a nation (V120, Ch16).

Abraham is revered by Muslims as the person who gave them their name as "Muslims" (i.e. those who believe in One God and submit to Him) (V78,Ch 22).

"Abraham was neither a Jew, nor a Christian; but he was "Musliman Hanifan" an upright man who had surrendered and sincerely submitted to Allah (God), and he was not of the idolaters"

The Holy Qur'an, V 67, Ch 3

Note : The origin of the name "Abraham" was Abram or Avram and it is written and pronounced "Ibrahim" in Arabic. The Roman Catholic Church calls Abraham "our father in Faith". The Eastern Orthodox Church commemorates him as the "Righteous Forefather Abraham".

It is believed that the first building of worshipping one God was established when Adam first descended on the earth. Muslims believe that the most important person who rebuilt this building and raised its walls was Prophet Abraham together with his son Ishmael. The building which is cubical in shape is called "Ka'bah". It is located in Mecca (Makkah) which is in the valley of Bacca (currently in Saudi Arabia). God imposed a duty upon Abraham and his son to purify the Ka'bah for those who pray, meditate and prostrate to Him. God made it a place of worship, and a sanctuary (a safe place and a resort) for the people.

Abraham and Ishmael's Supplication

> *"Our Lord! make us submissive unto You and of our Seed (descendants) a nation submissive unto You, and show us our ways (rites) of worship, and accept our repentance. You are the Most Forgiving the Most Merciful"*
>
> The Holy Qur'an, V 128, Ch 2

Hajj

Every year, more than three million Muslims perform pilgrimage "Hajj" to the Mosque of Sanctuary in Makkah (Mecca – Saudi Arabia). It is the fifth pillar of Islam that must be done once in a lifetime for those who have the financial and health capabilities to perform it.

Muhammad (pbuh) taught people how to perform Hajj, which mainly contains Abrahamic rites. He circumambulated (circulated or walked around the Kaaba) which is the cubical building established by Abraham as the House of God. Circulation is performed seven times and goes counterclockwise as an act of submission to God which is also harmonious with the motion of the planets and even the electrons.

Then he prayed behind Abraham's station. Currently it is an enclosure that contains Abraham's footprint on a piece of rock. (Muslims call it Maqam Ibrahim).

Then Muhammad (pbuh) walked between the Safa and Marwa hills, the same place Hagar walked thousands of years ago searching for water after her husband Abraham left her there with their son Ishmael. Abraham asked her to stay there as an act of obedience and submission to God's Command Who wanted the place to become a sanctuary and a place of worship.

The distance between these two hills is approximately 395 m. This Hajj rite is called Sa'ee i.e. a brisk walk between Safa and Marwa hills. It consists of 7 laps (with a total distance of 2.76 Km), starting from Safa and finishing at Marwa.

Sa'ee resembles the day to day motion, activity, actions, travel, effort and acts a person performs during his / her life. These acts and deeds must be for useful and value adding goals.

In addition to other Hajj rites, Muhammad (pbuh) went to a place currently known as "Jamarat" in a town called Mina (8 Km east of Makkah). There he threw stones in resemblance of Abraham's act, when he stoned the Satan who appeared to him as an old man trying to dissuade him from slaughtering his son as a sacrifice to God. Abraham stoned him several times. When Muslims perform the same act, they in fact challenge the Satan and the inner evil desires within themselves.

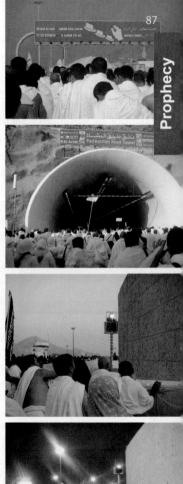

Finally, as God saved Abraham's son's life and instead substituted a ram, Muhammad (pbuh) taught Muslims to provide a sacrifice to God by slaughtering a sheep or a goat as a symbol of Abraham's sacrifice, and divide the meat among the poor.

Muhammad (pbuh) taught Muslims to dedicate a supplication for Abraham and his family in every prayer of the daily five prayers. Also, it is worth mentioning that Muhammad named one of his children "Ibrahim" who died at his childhood.

"Say (O Muhammad): My Lord has guided me to a straight path, a correct (right) religion, the way and community of Abraham, the upright way inclining towards the truth and he was not an idolater (he didn't associate others with God)"
The Holy Qur'an, V 161, Ch 6

It is believed that Abraham was buried in Hebron – Palestine. It is considered a sacred place for Jews, Christians and Muslims. The building complex that contains the cenotaph of Abraham is called "Al-Masjid Al-Ibrahimi" (Abraham's Mosque). Also called by non Muslims "Tombs of the Patriarchs".

The building is primarily a large mosque (rectangular shape) with two square minarets. It also includes many rooms and a series of subterranean caves.

The central room of the building contains the cenotaphs of Abraham and Sarah. The southern room (Ohel Yitzhak in Hebrew) contains the cenotaphs of Isaac and Rebecca.

Cenotaph of Abraham (pbuh)

Note: Muslims do not glorify tombs. According to Islamic teachings, the structure of the tomb must not be raised above the ground level.

The northern room of the building contains the cenotaphs of Jacob and Leah. It is widely believed the remnants of Abraham, Isaac, Jacob, Sarah, Rebecca, and Leah were enshrined in the subterranean chambers below the building.

The Man Who Spoke to God

Muhammad and Moses:
Muhammad (pbuh) praised highly the Prophet Moses and indicated that on the Day of Resurrection he will see Moses standing and holding the side of the Throne of God (Allah).

On another occasion when Muhammad (pbuh) came to Madinah and found that Jews fasted on the day of "Ashura" (which God saved the children of Israel from Pharaoh of Egypt), he asked Muslims to fast this day voluntarily because Moses fasted that day as an expression of thanks to God (The day of "Ashura" is on the 10th of the first month of the lunar calendar).

Approximately one third of the Holy Qur'an talks about Moses and the incidents and experiences the children of Israel went through. In addition, the Holy Quran mentions some of the prophets who were sent to the children of Israel such as Aaron, Zachariah and John.

The Holy Qur'an indicates that God spoke to Moses and describes Moses as one of five messengers and prophets who had heavy missions (Ulu Al Azm) and God took from them a solemn covenant (V8, Chapter 33 Al-Ahzab). The five messengers  are Noah, Abraham, Moses, Jesus and Muhammad peace be upon all of them.

Moses died near or at the mount Nebo which overlooks the Dead Sea and the land of Palestine. A memorial was built on the mount which became an important tourist attraction in Jordan.

حراسة الأراضي المقدسة
جبل نيبو - صياغة
مقام النبي موسى

MOUNT NEBO SIYAGHA
MEMORIAL OF MOSES

Muslims see many similarities between Moses and Muhammad. Both were prophets and messengers who brought a Divine Book that included the Law of God. Both lead their people and lived among them for a long period of time. Both married and had children.

Muhammad and Jesus:

According to authentic narrations Muhammad (pbuh) said:

> "I am the nearest of all the people to the son of Mary and all the prophets are paternal brothers, and there has been no prophet between me and him (i.e. Jesus)".

The Holy Qur'an describes Jesus as God's Word and glad tidings conveyed to Mary. His name is "The Messiah Jesus son of Mary".

Jesus in the Qur'an

God supported him with the Holy Spirit (Archangel Gabriel) and sent him as a messenger to the children of Israel to guide them to the straight path and to worship God "Allah" his Lord and their Lord and the Lord of all beings. (V87, Chapter 2, V 45-49, Chapter 3 ,V171, Chapter 4).

Nazareth is a historic town in lower Galilee, Palestine. Mentioned in the Gospels as the home of Mary, it is closely associated with the childhood of Jesus Christ. According to Roman Catholic tradition, Annunciation took place at the Church of the Annunciation in Nazareth.

Also, the Holy Qur'an describes Jesus as illustrious (memorable and prominent) in the world and the Hereafter, and one of the righteous and those brought near unto God.

The Holy Qur'an indicates that God taught Jesus the Scripture and wisdom, and the Torah and the Gospel. He supported him with miracles of healing the blind, and the leper, and raising the dead by His leave and Will (Allah Exalted be He).

Photos from Bethlehem: The Church of the Nativity is one of the oldest operating churches in the world. It is believed by many Christians it marks the birthplace of Jesus the Christ.

Muslims believe that Jesus will return. Muhammad (pbuh) indicated that the Day of Resurrection will not take place until Jesus descends from the heavens.

Jesus Return

He will return before life ends on the earth in order to establish the Law of God. He will fight the false Messiah, and unite all believers in God (Allah Exalted be He). He will be a just ruler and he will bring peace to the whole world. Muslims are required to be amongst the supporters of Jesus upon his return.

Photos from Damascus: According to some narrations, Prophet Muhammad (pbuh) indicated that Jesus will descend in the eastern side of Damascus.

Prophecy

Universality of the "Message" conveyed by Muhammad: Muslims believe that Muhammad received the same Message that was given to Abraham, Moses, Jesus and other prophets but his mission was universal. He was entrusted to correct people's beliefs, bring them back to the true faith and teach them good deeds.

> *"And We have not sent you but as a mercy to the worlds"*
> The Holy Qur'an, V 107, Ch 21

Muhammad's Letter to the Roman Emperor

Muhammad (pbuh) sent letters to the rulers and kings of neighbouring countries and superpowers such as Persia, Byzantine and Egypt calling them to accept Islam as "the Message of God". When Heraclius King of Byzantine received Muhammad's letter, he invited Abu-Sufyan (one of the main chiefs and tradesmen of Mecca who was by chance doing business in that area) to attend him. Heraclius asked Abu-Sufyan few questions and requested him to be honest.

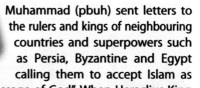

Letter of Prophet Muhammad (pbuh) to Heraclius (in original Arabic alphabets)

Heraclius	:	Which social class of the society does Muhammad come from?
Abu-Sufyan	:	He comes from a noble family in Mecca.
Heraclius	:	Did he ever betray, break a promise or lie?
Abu-Sufyan	:	No.
Heraclius	:	How about his followers, are they increasing or decreasing? And have any of his followers quit because he was unpleased with Muhammad?
Abu-Sufyan	:	In fact, Muhammad's followers admired him and they were increasing in number.
Heraclius	:	Then what does Muhammad teach his followers?
Abu-Sufyan	:	Belief in One God and social justice.

Heraclius thought for a while then he said: If what you told me is true, then Muhammad will be able to inherit my kingdom.

Emperor Heraclius ruled the Roman Empire from 610 to 640 CE during that time he conducted three military campaigns and defeated the Persian Empire and regained Syria, Palestine and Egypt. In year 636CE Islam reached Palestine, Syria, Egypt and most of Northern Africa. In the year 642 CE Islam reached Persia.

Islam, a universal religion: Currently Islam is the second largest religion in the world after Christianity. A comprehensive demographic study of more than 200 countries finds that there are 1.57 billion Muslims of all ages living in the world today, representing 23% of an estimated 2009 world population of 6.8 billion (Pew Forum on Religion & Public Life 2009).

Not all Muslims are Arabs: Arab Muslims constitute less than one fourth of the total number of Muslims in the world.

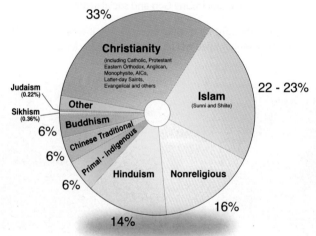

There is approximately 2.1 billion Christians in the world representing 33% of World's population and 1.1 billion non religious / atheist people in the world (16% of World's population). Judaism represents 0.22% of Worlds' population (approx 14 million people).

FOOTNOTES

1 Abstract from the story of Mary from the Holy Qur'an, Verses 16-23
Chapter 19 "Mary"

> *And mention Mary in the Scripture,*
> *when she had withdrawn from her people to an eastern place as a seclusion*
> *from them. Then We sent unto her Our spirit (Angel Gabriel) who appeared*
> *to her as a flawless human being.*
>
> *She said: I seek refuge from you to God, The Beneficent One if at all you*
> *fear Him.*
>
> *He said: I am none other than a messenger of your Lord to grant you a pure boy.*
>
> *She said: How shall I have a boy (son) and neither a human being has ever*
> *touched me nor have I been unchaste!*
>
> *He said: So (it will be). Your Lord said: It is easy for Me and We will make him*
> *a miraculous sign for all people and a Mercy from Us. It is a decreed matter.*
>
> *Soon she conceived him, and she hurried to a remote place but the birth pangs*
> *drove her unto the trunk of the palm tree. She said: Oh, I wish I had died before*
> *this and had become a thing utterly forgotten!*

According to the story mentioned in the Holy Qur'an, Mary brought her son to her own people who blamed her but Jesus (the newborn) miraculously spoke and said: Verses 30-35, Chapter 19 Mary:

> *Indeed, I am the servant of Allah. He (decreed) to give me the Scripture*
> *and make me a prophet and make me blessed wherever I may be. And He*
> *enjoined me to pray to him and give alms as long as I am alive and to be*
> *virtuous towards my mother. He didn't make me insolent or wretched. May*
> *all peace be upon me the day I was born and the day I will die and the day I*
> *shall be raised alive.*
>
> *That is Jesus son of Mary; it is the truth concerning what they doubt. It is not*
> *for God to take any son (Exalted Be He). When He decrees a matter, He but*
> *says to it : Be and so it is.*

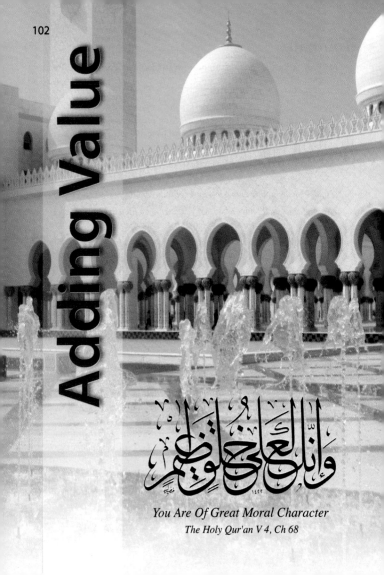

Adding Value

وَإِنَّكَ لَعَلَىٰ خُلُقٍ عَظِيمٍ

You Are Of Great Moral Character

The Holy Qur'an V 4, Ch 68

Adding Value to People's Lives

Adding Value

Muhammad encouraged people to love each other:

Muhammad (pbuh) said: "I swear by God that you will not be true believers in Him unless you love each other. I will tell you something if you do it you will love each other. Greet each other frequently and make it a common habit.

And he said: "No one will become a good believer unless he wishes for his brethrens what he likes for himself".

Also said: "Whoever helps a believer overcome a difficulty, God will help him overcome a difficulty at the Day of Judgment, and God will always help an individual as long as he/she is helping others" [1].

Meeting others with a bright smiling face is an act of charity.

Muhammad (pbuh)

Greeting people is a message of peace: Muhammad (pbuh) said: "Don't ever underestimate any kind act, even if you meet others with a bright (smiling) face"[2]. And he said: "The one who greets others first is closer to God than the others"[3]. On another occasion he said to someone who asked him about a good way to deal with people: "Offer people food and greet whom you know and whom you don't know". [4]

Muhammad used to greet people warmly: According to authentic narrations, Muhammad used to meet people with a bright face and when he shook hands with others, he never released his hand before the other person.

Muhammad had a high sense of humour: He was a very cheerful and optimistic person. People who dealt with him described him as a likable person and at the same time he was venerated and respected.

On several occasions he joked with his friends, his wife, old people and children (including his own children and grandchildren). At Muhammad's time, racing (as running) was a common activity to have fun. It was narrated that Muhammad (pbuh) was seen several times racing with his wife, his children and other children.

High sense of humour with an old woman: It was narrated that an old woman asked him to pray for her so that she would enter God's paradise. Muhammad (pbuh) replied in a non serious way: "There are no old women in God's Paradise". She misunderstood what he said and got confused. But soon he elaborated: "You

will be young when you enter the Paradise (and all people will be). 🙂

High sense of humour with his friends: One time, Muhammad (pbuh) saw a sore-eyed person named Suhayb (who was a Roman Muslim), looking miserable and was eating a ripe date. Muhammad (pbuh) wanted to joke with him in order to cheer him up so he said to him: "How come you eat the date and your left eye is sore?". Suhayb realised that Muhammad was joking with him so he replied: "Don't worry I am eating it on the right side of my mouth (the side where the right eye was sound).

Anas Bin Malek narrated that a man came to Muhammad and asked him to give him a ride on a camel. Muhammad (pbuh) said: I will give you a ride on the child of the she camel. The man replied: What am I going to do with the camel's child? Then Muhammad said: Are not all camels the children of she camels?5

Muhammad cared for and loved children: Muhammad paid attention to children. He used to greet them and play with them. One time Muhammad (pbuh) saw a little boy who was sad because his little bird died. Although Muhammad (pbuh) was heading elsewhere, he spent some time with the little boy to please him and relieve his sadness.6

Muhammad (pbuh) used to ask parents to express their love to their children by kissing and hugging them and being fair with all their children.

Muhammad (pbuh) described a father who never kissed his child as lacking mercy in his heart.

Muhammad loved his neighbours: Muhammad had a Jewish neighbour who did not accept Islam and was not

kind to him. When the Jewish neighbour became sick, Muhammad (pbuh) visited him at his home, which softened his neighbour's heart. Also, Muhammad (pbuh) visited a Jewish boy at his home when he became sick because the boy had worked for some time as a helper or a servant for Muhammad (pbuh).

Muhammad emphasised kindness to neighbours: Muhammad (pbuh) told his companions that Archangel Gabriel emphasized on being good to neighbours to the extent that Muhammad (pbuh) thought that a person would be able to inherit from his/ her neighbours. Muhammad (pbuh) stated that whoever believes in God and the Day of Judgment should be kind to his / her neighbours. On one occasion he said to a companion called "Abu-Thar": "If you cook soup, cook it with more water (i.e. increase its quantity) so that it becomes enough to give some to your neighbours".

Muhammad abolished bad social manners: He stated on several occasions "the people of good morals are the closest to him on the Day of Judgment and will be most beloved by him". Also he stated:

"Don't hate each other and don't envy each other and be brothers". [7]

"A believer in God does not curse or swear or use bad language". [8]

No derision or defamation: Muhammad (pbuh) recited the following verses from the Holy Qur'an (considered by Muslims as God's Words not Muhammad's own words).

"O believers, don't disdain (or ridicule or deride) each other neither men deride men nor women deride women, the latter could be better than the former.

"Don't defame one another and don't insult one another and whoever does so and does not repent to Allah he or she is indeed a wrongdoer"

The Holy Qur'an, V 11, Ch 49

No ill opinion, evil suspicion, spying and backbiting:

> "O believers,
> avoid much suspicion, for some suspicion is a grave
> (serious) sin and don't spy on one another, nor backbite
> against one another.
> Would any of you like to eat the flesh of his dead brother?
> You would hate it. So fear Allah (God), He is the Most
> Forgiving the Most Merciful."
>
> The Holy Qur'an, V 12, Ch 49

Don't pass wrong news:

> "O believers,
> if a transgressor brings you some news (that may require
> taking action then verify it carefully before you believe him
> or her and act upon it, so you don't harm people in ignorance
> and then become regretful for what you have done".
>
> The Holy Qur'an, V 6-7, Ch 49

Don't cheat and be honest: Trading, buying and selling should be based on ethics and should comply with noble values such as honesty, perfection, transparency and cooperation. Muhammad (pbuh) said:

> "Whoever cheats is not one amongst us"
> (i.e. among the righteous believers).
>
> Narrated by Muslim, Abu Dawood

Adding Value

Lying or breaking a promise is hypocrisy:

NO Hypocrisy

Muhammad (pbuh) said:

"Whoever has the following four (characteristics) will be a hypocrite and whoever has one of them will have one characteristic of hypocrisy until he gives it up:

❶ Whenever he is entrusted, he betrays;
❷ Whenever he speaks, he tells a lie;
❸ Whenever he makes a covenant, he proves treacherous;
❹ Whenever he quarrels, he behaves in a very imprudent, evil and insulting manner."

Muhammad condemned extremism: He called for a balanced way of life, balanced views and rational thinking. It is narrated that three people came to his house to ask about his style of worship. Muhammad (pbuh) wasn't at home and his wife spoke with them. They found his level of worship to be less than what they expected to be practiced by a Prophet.

According to their understanding, religious way of life requires focusing on spiritualities and ignoring some of the body needs or depriving it it from natural desires.

They thought that they need to stay single and must not get married. Also, a person needs to fast every day and perform extra prayers late at night besides the daily prayers (i.e. permanent change in eating habits and life style).

When Muhammad (pbuh) knew what they said, he was upset but he stated that he usually performed extra prayers at night and rested like other people. In addition to the annual fasting in the month of Ramadan, he fasted for some time and he did not fast for other times.

Finally, he got married and did not like people to stay single. He said:

"This is my Sunnah (the way of life that God likes). Whoever does not accept it, he / she is not one of us".

Perfect balance in satisfying body and soul needs: On several occasions, Muhammad (pbuh) called for maintaining the right balance between materialism and spiritualism. Body and soul's needs must be satisfied in moderation and in lawful ways.

Body & Soul

He encouraged people to take religion as a change to a better and easier way of life not to a harder and stricter way of life.

Also, he encouraged people to look after their bodies and eat in moderation.

Muhammad does not like hardship: It is narrated that whenever Muhammad (pbuh) had to decide on a matter or an issue where more than one option or alternative was given, he always avoided hardship and chose less complicated ones provided that it fullfilled the required goals and did not involve unlawful things.

Simplicity

Adding value through sport:

Muhammad (pbuh) used to encourage his companions to maintain healthy bodies and learn different types of sports such as swimming, archery, horse riding and horse racing (horsemanship).

In addition he participated in several running competitions with his companions, a sport that brings happiness and excitement. It is narrated that Muhammad (pbuh) used to do running races with his wife Aisha. She won the race once and he won the race on another occasion. This activity reflects the mutual love, harmony and fun Muhammad (pbuh) had with his wife.

Muhammad (pbuh) allocated an area to be a racing field in the western side of the Nabawi Mosque in Madinah. Horse racing used to be conducted in the

same field as well. A mosque was built next to the racing field and it was called the Sabaq Mosque (i.e. the mosque of the racing field).

Adding value through knowledge:

Muhammad (pbuh) brought a Message of light and guidance that became the source for civilization and scientific advancement for many centuries. It commenced from a divine revelation that had begun with the word "Read". Within decades, it revolutionized knowledge and all types of sciences in Arabia and the whole world.

The words: read, think, learn, observe, explore, understand, ponder, contemplate, see and reflect are frequently mentioned in the Holy Qur'an.

> *Indeed, in the creation of the heavens and the earth and in the alteration of the night and the daylight are signs (of God's creative power) for those of understanding and discretion. The ones who remember Allah (the Lord of all beings) with reverence while standing and while sitting and while lying on their sides. And who reflect on the creation of the heavens and the earth, and say:*
> *Our Lord! You have not created all this in vain, exalted are You, then protect us from the punishment of the Fire.*
>
> The Holy Qur'an V190,191, Ch 3

> *And in the earth, there are wondrous (incredible) signs (indicating the presence of God) and in yourselves (there are similar signs), can you not then see?*
>
> The Holy Qur'an V20, 21 Ch 51

Muhammad (pbuh) added value to peoples' lives by encouraging them to learn and seek useful knowledge. He urged his companions to utilize knowledge for the wellbeing of humanity and not to cause mischief on the earth. He linked that to God's pleasure when he said:

> "That who follows a way for acquiring knowledge, God facilitates a way for him to Paradise"
>
> Narrated by Tirmithi

For many centuries, Muslim scientists were the frontiers in pure and applied sciences. The language of Qur'an "Arabic" became the language of sciences that were taught in full-fledged universities granting degrees in chemistry, mathematics, calculus, medicine, astronomy, geography, engineering, art and literature.

Some researchers acknowledge the truth that the western civilization relied primarily on the Islamic civilization. Without it, the western civilization would need at least 500 years to accomplish what it has already achieved.

Table 2: Contributions of famous Muslim Scientists

Adding Value

Scientist	Major Contributions
Algoritmi Father of Algorithms 780-850 CE	**Mohammad Ibn Musa Al-Khwarizmi** was one of the greatest scientists of his time. He was a mathematician, an astronomer and a geographer. He introduced the decimal positional number system to the world. He made a great contribution to Mathematics when he developed Algebra (derived from the word Al-Jabr) and "algorithms" who gave his name to it. His name is the origin of the word guarismo in Spanish and the word algarismo in Portuguese, both meaning digit.
Geber Father of Chemistry 721-815 CE	**Jaber Ibn Hayyan** was a prominent polymath: a chemist, astronomer, astrologer, engineer, geologist, philosopher, physicist, and pharmacist and physician. He is considered by many scientists to be the father of chemistry. He was the first to discover many acids such as nitric, hydrochloric and sulfuric acids. He described many chemical processes such as evaporation, sublimation and distillation. The historian of chemistry Erick John Holmyard gives credit to Geber for developing alchemy into an experimental science.
Rhases (Rasis) Father of Physicians 865-929 CE	**Abu Bakr Muhammad Ibn Zakariya Al-Razi**. He was considered by many scientists as the father of physicians. He was the first to differentiate smallpox from measles. He discovered numerous compounds and chemicals including alcohol and kerosene. Edward Granville Browne considers him as the most original of all the physicians. He wrote many important books which were translated to different languages including English such as "Al-Hawi" medical Encyclopedia, The Big Pharmacology, Kidney and Bladder Stones and The Book of Experiences.

Avicenna Father of Modern Medicine 980-1307 CE	**Abu Ali Al-Hussein Ibn Sina** is one of the most eminent Muslim scholars in medicine and one of the most famous Muslim scientists in the world. He was a polymath and the author of almost 200 books on science, religion and philosophy.
	Avicenna's two most important works are: Shifa (The Book of Healing) which is a philosophical encyclopedia based on Aristotelian tradition and Al Qanun Fi-Tibb (The Canon of Medicine).
	The Canon is a 14-volume book classifies and describes diseases, and outlines their assumed causes. It was translated to different languages and was a standard medical text in Europe for seven centuries (until early 18th century).
Al Jazari 1136-1206 CE	**Abul-Iz Bin Ismael Al-Jazari**. He is best known for writing the "Book of Knowledge of Ingenious Mechanical Devices" where he described fifty mechanical devices along with instructions on how to construct them.
	Al-Jazari's is also known as the inventor of the largest astronomical "castle clock", which is considered to be the first programmable analog computer.
	According to Donald Routledge Hill, Al-Jazari described the most sophisticated candle clocks. He also invented the water clock and the crank shaft that transforms rotary motion into linear motion.

Avicenna

LATIN FIGURES:

I, II, III, IV, V, VI, VII, VIII, IX, X

ARABIC NUMBERS :

1, 2, 3, 4, 5, 6, 7, 8, 9, 10

Adding Value

Adding value to trade and commerce:

Muhammad (pbuh) encouraged trade and commerce based on noble Islamic values that denounce cheating, unethical dealings, deception, fraud, monopoly and exploitation.

Free Trade Zone

Muhammad (pbuh) indicated:

> God bestows His mercy on a person who is tolerant when he buys, tolerant when he sells and tolerant when he asks for his rights. *(Applicable for males and females - Bukhari, 2076/16)*

Soon after he arrived in Madinah, Muhammad instructed his companions to buy a piece of land and dedicate it for free trade. People used to buy and sell in it without paying any fees or custom charges. They called it Manakha.

Manakha means the place where camels are seated on the ground in order to offload goods carried on their backs (for trade purposes).

Other markets in Madinah - present time

The land had been left as an endowment until now. The following picture shows the wall surrounding the land of free trade.

Adding value through etiquette:

Muhammad (pbuh) cared for behavioral etiquette. He taught his companions that etiquette is part of his example and way of life (Sunnah). In addition, many verses in the Holy Qur'an urge on tenderness and good manners. Muhammad (pbuh) indicated that Angels get upset by what upsets human beings. (e.g. loud voices, bad smells, etc.)

The following points summarize some of the Islamic behavioral etiquettes:

- Do not talk loudly and do not walk arrogantly.

- Do not stay long when visiting a sick person, give him or her time to rest.

- One should smell good when he/she comes to the mosque.

- Those who ate garlic or onion should not come to the mosque, so as not to disturb the others by any unfavorable smell or act (e.g. burping).

- Be helpful and give space to others in crowded and congregation areas where finding a free space is difficult.

- Call others with the names and nicknames they like.

- Put your hand on your mouth when yawning and bless others when they sneeze.

- When talking to others, one should use the best and the most acceptable words to them so as they like it. The good word is alms (charity) in Islam.

- Talk kindly to your parents and don't shout at their faces, never say a bad word even "uff or fie" (the smallest negative word in Arabic).

- Children should always knock on the door and seek permission to enter, before going into their parents' room at certain times during the day.

- If you are serving water to others, you are the last one to drink (a preferred etiquette).

- If you are invited for a dinner or a banquet, eat from the closer pots to you and don't annoy the others.

- Don't breath in a cup of water while drinking from it.

Etiquette with Women

Lower your gaze, don't stare at women or at passing people.

Muhammad (pbuh) was seen bending his knees for his wife Safiya to help her climb first on the camel by stepping on his thigh.

(Narrated by Anas bin Malek – Bukhari - 9/20)

Purification and cleanliness:

Cleanliness and personal hygiene are essential elements in the Islamic faith. Verse 222, Chapter 2 in the Holy Qur'an states that God loves those who purify themselves.

> *"...Truly, Allah loves those who turn unto Him in repentance and loves those who purify themselves (physically and spiritually)".*
>
> The Holy Qur'an, V 222, Ch 2

> *"And your clothing purify."*
>
> The Holy Qur'an, V 4, Ch 74

Ablution Everyday

Performing ablution before praying is an essential requirement for prayers. It includes washing the hands, face, forearms up to the elbows, wiping the head and washing the feet.

In addition, performing "Ghusul" (washing the whole body) on a regular basis is strongly recommended and is considered as part of Muhammad's Sunnah (teachings and way of life). However, Ghusul is a must for purity on certain occasions (e.g. after marital contact and menstruation).

Muhammad (pbuh) emphasized cleanliness and purification in all aspects of life. He asked his companions to clean their homes and surroundings regularly. He taught them that removing harm or garbage from the road is a rewardable charity act.

Also, Muhammad (pbuh) urged his companions to maintain high personal hygiene and cleanliness. His sayings in this context indicate the following:

- Dress in clean and tidy clothes but do not be prodigal
- Use perfumes (Teeb) to smell good
- Trim your nails, remove pubic and armpit hair
- Wash hands before and after eating. Do not touch food after waking up until hands are washed.

Adding Value

Cleanliness is next to Godliness

Cleanliness or purification is half of the faith.

Muhammad (pbuh)
Sahih Muslim and Tirmithi

Miswak and dental care. Clean mouth and good breath during the whole day:

Dental Care

According to authentic narrations Muhammad (pbuh) said:

> "If it did not trouble you, I would ask you to brush your teeth with miswak before each prayer." (five times a day)
> (Narrated by Bukhari & Muslim)

What is miswak ?

Miswak is a common name for Salvadore persica (tooth brush tree, also known as the Arak tree). It is popularly used in Saudi Arabia. Miswak wicks clean between the teeth and do not break under pressure, rather they are flexible and strong.

The chemical analysis of Miswak shows that it contains many useful minerals and elements such as fluorides in large amounts, silica, vitamin C and small quantities of chlorides, tannins, saponins, flavenoids and sterols.

According to analytical research, Miswak helps fight plaques, recession and bleeding of gums. The Miswak stick releases fresh sap and silica (hard glossy material) which acts as an abrasive material to remove stains. Miswak can clean teeth gently and effectively, whitens the teeth without harming enamel or gum.

The chloride content helps remove the plaque and tartar stains and vitamin C contributes to the healing and repair of the tissues. It is believed that Miswak extract relieves head ache, common cold, nausea, tensions, and dizziness.

Muhammad (pbuh) used to respect others' views:

Whenever he gave instructions to his followers that were understood or perceived in two different ways, he used to accept both ways provided that both of them achieve the required goal in a lawful manner.

In the battle of "That Al-Salassel", the Muslim Commander Amr Bin Al-Aass was criticised for leading a prayer without performing ghusul and ablution (he was in a state of spiritual impurity). Muhammad (pbuh) listened to his justification and accepted it. Amr told Muhammad (pbuh) that it was cold that night and if he showered his body, he could fall sick and could not lead his group.

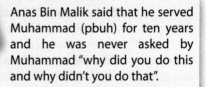

Anas Bin Malik said that he served Muhammad (pbuh) for ten years and he was never asked by Muhammad "why did you do this and why didn't you do that".

Muhammad encouraged consultancy and democracy (Shura): Muhammad (pbuh) always consulted his companions and even his wife. He advised his followers to be objective and use rational thinking. He empowered them and involved them in the decision making process.

When the Meccan chiefs, along with other Arab tribes, planned to attack Madinah, a Persian Muslim put forward a proposal to dig a trench on the northern side of Madinah.

Consultancy

Although that was a foreign concept never applied before in Arabia and it was put forward by an ordinary person, Muhammad (pbuh) considered it seriously and it was approved by the majority of Muslims. They dug a trench 5.5 km long x 4.6 m wide.

On another occasion, (battle of Badr) a commoner (an ordinary person) told Muhammad: "O Prophet, if your choice to camp in this area is not inspired by a revelation, can I suggest we move to another area?". The person put forward the reasons for his suggestion and after consultations, Muhammad (pbuh) welcomed the proposal likewise the majority of Muslims; they moved to the other area.

The word Muhammad in Arabic being designed in an artistic way. Courtesy of Artist Farid Al-Ali.

Respect people of other faiths: Muhammad (pbuh) encouraged his companions to be friendly and transparent with people of other faiths while maintaining an assertive personality and clear understanding about their Islamic faith.

Muhammad (pbuh) demonstrated how highly he respected people regardless of their faith in several occasions. It is narrated that he stood up showing respect for a funeral carrying a coffin of a Jewish man that passed him and his companions. Muhammad answered a companion who wondered why Muhammad (pbuh) stood up for the carried body: "He is a human being" (regardless of his race, faith and social class).

Interfaith dialogue and peaceful coexistance with people of other faiths: Interfaith dialogue can be defined as a two way communication

Interfaith Dialogue

or discussion between people of different religious faiths and traditions in order to reach positive outcomes such as moving from suspicion and confusion to understanding and awareness or from hostility to friendliness.

Grand Mufti of Bosnia Dr Mustafa Ceric and Bishop Kevin Manning, Catholic Diocese of Parramatta. Sydney Australia 2007

In the year 632 CE, Muhammad (pbuh) received and hosted at his mosque in the city of "Madinah" a Christian delegation who came from Najran (in Yemen) to learn about Islam and discuss the differences between Islam and Christianity.

Dialogue with a Christian Delegation

Muhammad (pbuh) set guidelines and etiquettes for dialogue and debate with others based on the Quranic teachings which emphasize respect, wisdom, mutual understanding and kindness. He recited the following verses from the Holy Qur'an :

> *"Call (invite people) to the Way of your Lord with wisdom and with "good admonition" and reason (debate) with them in the best manner. Your Lord Knows best who strayed from His Path and who received (able to receive) guidance."*
>
> The Holy Qur'an, V 125, Ch 16

> *"And do not debate with the People of the Book except with the best manner unless those of them who were aggressors (unjust or exceeded just limits). Say (to them): we believe in what has been revealed to us and what has been revealed to you; our God and your God is One, and to Him we are submitting."*
>
> The Holy Qur'an, V 46, Ch 29

Religious Tolerance

Omar Mosque and the Church of the Holy Sepulcher, Jerusalem:

In the old city of Jerusalem, a great example of religious tolerance has been existing for many centuries. It started when the second Muslim ruler of the Islamic state Caliph Omar Bin Al-Khattab took over Jerusalem (638 CE) peacefully without shedding a drop of blood.

Omar was invited by the Archbishop of Jerusalem, Sophronius, to pray in the Church of the Holy Sepulcher. The Church is also known as the Church of the Resurrection

(Anastasis to Eastern Orthodox Christians). It is the holiest Christian site in the world. It encompasses Calvary where the Christians believe Jesus was crucified, and the tomb (sepulcher) where he was buried. It has been an important pilgrimage destination since the 4th century, C.E.

In a remarkable gesture, Omar refused to pray in the Church, saying: **"If I had prayed in the church it would have been taken by Muslims as a mosque or a worship place".**

Omar instead prayed a few yards outside the church. His act confirmed the peaceful coexistence between Islam and other religions. It confirmed freedom of worship for non Muslims under the Islamic state.

A mosque was built on that site where Omar prayed to commemorate this historical event (later, it was called Omar Mosque).

Caliph Omar entrusted the custody of the Church of the Holy Sepulchre, to 'Ubadah Ibn Al-Samit, a companion of prophet Muhammad (pbuh) who became the first Muslim judge of Jerusalem. Ubadah died in the year 658CE and was buried in the "Gate of Mercy" cemetery at the southern corner of the wall enclosing the Noble Sanctuary. The Sanctuary includes the Dome of the Rock and Aqsa Mosque.

Tomb of Ubadah Ibn Al-Samit in Jerusalem

The Covenant of Omar:

Omar granted the people of Jerusalem a covenant of peace and protection which came to be known the "Covenant of Omar". It has been mounted at the door of the mosque along the centuries and until now.

The Covenant of Omar

In the Name of (God) Allah, the Most Merciful, the Most Compassionate

This is an assurance of peace and protection given by the servant of Allah Omar to the people of Ilia' (Jerusalem). He gave them an assurance of protection for their lives, property, churches as well as the sick and healthy and all its religious community.

Their churches shall not be occupied, demolished nor taken away wholly or in part. They shall neither be coerced in their religion nor shall any of them be injured. The people of Ilia shall pay tax (Jizia) as inhabitants of cities do (and as Muslims do pay a similar tax "zakat").

FOOTNOTES

1   Riyadh Al-Salihin (183/3), (245/2), Sahih Al-Bukhari (13)
2   Riyadh Al-Salihin (121/5)
3   Riyadh Al-Salihin (858/2)
4   Sahih Al-Bukhari (11)
5   Sahih Al Albani, Abu Dawood, Emam Ahmed and Trimithi
6   Riyadh Al-Salihin (862/1), Bukhari (598/10)
7   Riyadh Al-Salihin (1591/1), Sahih Al-Bukhari (6065)
8   Riyadh Al-Salihin (1734/1) (1738/3)

Women

Blue Mosque, Istanbul, Turkey

Muhammad Gave Women Their Rights

Before the advent of Islam, women had no civil rights. Arabs used to give preference to male babies over female ones to the extent that many fathers used to bury their female babies or children alive.

No gender discrimination: Muhammad (pbuh) condemned discrimination between male and female children and taught his companions to love their children and raise them properly regardless of their sex. In fact, he emphasised giving more care and attention to female children until they grow up and get married. Muhammad (pbuh) said:

> "Women are the twin halves of men." [1]

Women inherit like men: Before Islam, women had no right to inherit. Muhammad successfully changed this custom. Females gained the right to inherit like males. However, Muhammad (pbuh) did not create the Islamic inheritance system, but he conveyed God's Words (preserved in the Holy Qur'an) which stipulate the portions for each individual (male and female) eligible to inherit.

The word "Muhammad" in Arabic calligrphy being designed in an artistic and symmetrical way. The actual word looks like this مُحَمَّد . Letters M and H (which form the first half of the word "Muhammad" are symmetrical with letters M and D (which form the second half of the word "Muhammad" in Arabic.

Women have a unique identity: A wife is not considered part of her husband's belongings. She is a free person who has a unique identity. When a woman gets married, she does not need to change her surname. Her identity is preserved and her wealth and property are protected by the Islamic law. When her husband passes away, she is considered as one of the heirs and not a property that is inherited by male heirs as it had been before Islam. (Before Islam, women were treated as chattel).

A woman is not a sex tool: Prostitution and adultery are strictly forbidden in Islam. Muhammad (pbuh) indicated: When a person commits fornication or adultery then he/she is not in a state of "Eaman" (faithfulness) (i.e. faith in God has not yet established strongly in his/her heart, therefore the person does not feel guilty or fear God when fornication is committed). God revealed in the Holy Qur'an:

> *"And don't approach (come near unto) fornication (unlawful premarital or extramarital sex), Lo! It is an abomination and an evil way".*
>
> The Holy Qur'an, V 32, Ch 17

sexual harassment sexual harassment illegitimate children nudity AIDS sexual diseases non-marital s nudity pornography nudity pornograph nudity sexual assault nudity pornography sexual assault sexual harassme sexual assault rape crimes sexual harass non-marital sex sexual diseases illegitimate children rape crimes sexual harassment sexual assa

In Islam, wearing headscarf and modest clothing is an obligation on adult women. In addition, Islamic teachings forbid women from using their bodies or femininity for public leisure and sexual temptation.

Businesses, commercials and advertisements that rely on exposing women bodies for temptation and sexual attraction are not allowed in Islam.

Islamic teachings block out the means that could lead to sexual harassment, sexual assault, rape crimes, sexual diseases, and other abominations such as nudity and pornography.

Get married!

Muhammad (pbuh) encouraged people to get married and establish a family life. He taught his followers noble Islamic values which ban illegal sexual relations other than a normal marital relationship between a man and a woman.

Non Marital Sex

A young man asked Muhammad (pbuh) to give him permission to fornicate (have non-marital sex with a girlfriend or a prostitute), Muhammad replied: "Do you accept this for your mother?". The man answered: "No". Muhammad (pbuh) said: "Likewise people don't like it for their mothers".

Then he asked the young man the same question three more times: "Do you like it for your daughter, sister, aunt?". Every time the man replied no and Muhammad (pbuh) repeated the same statement: "Likewise, people don't like it for their daughters, sisters and aunts".

Then Muhammad (pbuh) put his hand on the man's heart and supplicated to God: "Oh my Lord: forgive his sin, purify his heart and grant him chastity".

Muhammad empowered women:

Within his endeavours to empower women's role in the society, Muhammad (pbuh) allocated certain days every week for women education.

He urged them to participate in Islamic events, feasts and prayers. Even housemaids could meet Muhammad (pbuh), talk to him and seek for his help or advice.

He also asked women to do a formal pledge (as men did) since they were responsible to the Islamic law.

Women play a crucial role in society as they nurture and raise the next generation who will form the nation. Muslim women were empowered to take an active role in the society without overlapping men's role.

Although priority was always given to the task of raising children and caring for their wellbeing, women used to work and participate in the social and political life.

Muhammad encouraged caring for girls/daughters:

Muhammad (pbuh) emphasised on several occasions the good treatment of females and he described them as delicate and "as fragile as glass". He told his companions that whoever raises his daughters properly and fears God in caring for them and guiding them to faith, he will gain Paradise.

Muhammad encouraged full respect of mothers: A man asked Muhammad (pbuh): "Who would deserve my closest support and companionship? Muhammad replied: "Your mother". Then the man asked Muhammad (pbuh) who will be after her? Muhammad (pbuh) replied: "Your mother".

The man asked the same question again and Muhammad (pbuh) replied for the third time: "Your mother". Then out of curiosity the man asked the same question for the fourth time (he realised that Muhammad wanted to emphasise the best treatment to mothers). Then Muhammad (pbuh) said to him: "Your father" (i.e. your father deserves your closest support and accompany after your mother)[2].

Scholars comment on the above story that mothers can not escape three main sufferings " (1) pregnancy, (2) labor and delivery, (3) and finally breastfeeding and weaning.

Muhammad encouraged good treatment of wives : He stated that if a man disliked one of a woman's traits he will be pleased with another. And he said:

The believers who show the most perfect faith are those who have the best character; and the best of the believers are those who are best to their wives.

This promotes love, harmony and mutual understanding.

On the other hand Muhammad (pbuh) disliked divorce; he pointed out:

Divorce

Women

"Among all the permitted acts, divorce is the most hateful to God".

Should divorce become unavoidable, separation should be on good terms and with kindness [3].

Muhammad loved his wife: Few years after his first wife Khadijah passed away, Muhammad got married to Aisha

the daughter of his closest friend Abu-Bakir. Despite his loyalty to his late wife, he loved Aisha and was honest to her. He was asked once by Amr bin Al-Aass (a companion): "Who is the most beloved person to you?". Muhammad (pbuh) replied without hesitation: Aisha.

Confirm your love to your wife: Aisha narrated that Muhammad (pbuh) described his love for her like a knot firmly tied in a rope. Aisha used to ask Muhammad from time to time "how is the knot" and Muhammad (pbuh) used to confirm his love to her. He said: "the knot is still tied as firmly as it used to be".

Muhammad (pbuh) used to ask Aisha to send a serving of food to the friends of his late wife Khadijah every time Aisha cooked a sheep or an ewe.

Be a Loyal Husband

Muhammad mentioned to Aisha that no one was better than Khadijah at her time, she believed him when he first received God's revelation but many people did not (*some of his uncles and relatives did not believe him*). She consoled him with her money and supported him without hesitation.

Despite the fact that some people may view Muhammad's comments about his late wife Khadijah as it was triggering jealousy in his current wife Aisha, he was a fair and a loyal husband to his wives.

Muhammad demonstrated exemplar loyalty to his late wife:
According to some narrations, when Muhammad (pbuh) returned to Mecca in the year 630 CE, he asked his companions to pitch his tent near the grave of Khadijah. That was an expression of love and loyalty to her.

This is the word "Muhammad" in Arabic being designed in a formative style which looks like a flower. Courtesy of Plastic Artist Farid Al-Ali.

Muhammad and Polygamy

Muhammad did not introduce polygamy: In fact polygamy existed before Islam without any limit in number. It was very common for a man to have more than one woman either as wives or as concubines or slaves[4].

It is known that Prophet Abraham was married to Sara the mother of Isaac and Hagar the mother of Ishmael. Also, it is narrated that Jacob had four women, two wives and two concubines[5] (Genesis 32:23-24).

Muhammad lived most of his life married to one woman: He was married to Khadijah for almost 25 years and he was a father for 4 girls and 2 boys. Both of his sons died in their childhood.

After Khadijah passed away he married a poor old widow called "Sawdah". Her husband passed away after they returned from Abyssinia, the country which Muhammad (pbuh) sent some of his companions to seek refuge.

His marriage to Sawdah was a form of support for her. Muhammad (pbuh) was almost 50 years old when he married Sawdah who was older than him.

Muhammad married the daughter of his closest companion Abu-Bakir : Few years later, Muhammad (pbuh) married Aisha, the daughter of his closest friend and most supportive companion Abu-Bakir. The marriage was an honour for Abu-Bakir and Aisha.

Muhammad married the daughter of his second closest companion Omar : Two years later, Hafsa the daughter of his second closest companion Omar, lost her husband in the battle of Uhud and became a widow. Omar preferred that his daughter gets married to one of his trusted

friends but no one proposed to her. Then Muhammad (pbuh) took the initiative and proposed to her. The marriage was an honour and support for Omar and his daughter Hafsa.

Muhammad married a Muslim widow who was the daughter of his enemy: Ramlah was known by the nick name "Um Habibah". She was the daughter of the top man in Mecca (Abu-Sufyan). Although Abu-Sufyan did not believe Muhammad and fought him for 20 years, his daughter embraced Islam.

She was one of the early Muslims who migrated to Abyssinia with her husband and lived there for almost 15 years.

Her husband converted to Christianity and passed away there. She was left alone in Abyssinia, so Muhammad (pbuh) proposed to Um Habibah and she accepted and got married to him. Surprisingly, one year later, her father embraced Islam.

Muhammad married Safiyya, a woman from a Jewish tribe: Bani Al-Nadhir was one of the Jewish tribes who betrayed Muhammad (pbuh) and worked against him. After Muhammad (pbuh) besieged them in their city Khaybar, they surrendered.

Safiyya the daughter of their leader was amongst those who were captured. Muhammad (pbuh) released her and proposed marriage to her. Safiyya accepted and they were married.

Muhammad (pbuh) proved to all people that he had nothing against the Jewish community but aggressors had to be stopped regardless of their race or faith.

On several occasions and even after Muhammad (pbuh) passed away, Safiyya described him as a loving and a fair husband.

Mariya the copt:

In the same year, Muhammad (pbuh) sent a messenger to the ruler of Egypt who was Christian, calling him to accept the message of Islam.

The ruler of Egypt replied with a polite apology and sent Muhammad some gifts as well as a physician and a servant or concubine called Mariya (Mary). Muhammad (pbuh) accepted the Egyptian ruler's gifts. He married Mariya and later on she gave birth to a baby boy named Ibrahim. Ibrahim died when he was a little boy and Muhammad (pbuh) was very sad about losing him[6].

Muhammad conveyed God's Command to control polygamy: Islam didn't forbid polygamy but it restricted and regulated it. In Islam, it is not compulsory to marry more than one wife but it is permissible for genuine reasons.

A man can marry a second wife if he can demonstrate full respect, justice and impartiality to his wives. Verse 3, Chapter 4 in the Holy Qur'an indicates clearly that a man cannot marry more than one woman if he cannot treat them rightly and impartially.

God's Word

If you cannot be fair, marry only 1

Also, the verse puts a limit of four wives only for unbiased and fair husbands.

Before this revelation, men used to have scores of wives with no limits or conditions.

Limits on Prophet Muhammad: Prophet Muhammad (pbuh) was married to more than 4 wives before this revelation. Being wives of the "Messenger of God" was a great honour to them besides their being regarded as the mothers of believers. God revealed in the Holy Qur'an that Muhammad's wives were lawful to him. However, no more women could be married to Prophet Muhammad (pbuh) even if he divorced any of his wives.[7]

Limits on prophet Muhammad's wives:
Muslims were not allowed to marry any of the wives of Prophet Muhammad (pbuh) after he passed away because they were like their mothers.

In the Holy Qur'an, God described the wives of the Prophet as being unlike other women (they should be seen by other Muslims as exemplary and as the mothers of believers).

If any of the Prophet's wives committed a manifestly sinful deed, the punishment would be doubled for her. But if any of the Prophet's wives devoutly obeyed God and His Messenger and performed righteous deeds, she would receive double rewards.

Muhammad's wives had freedom of choice:
God asked Muhammad (as indicated in the Holy Qur'an, chapter 33 verses 28,29) to give his wives two options, either be released (i.e. divorced) if any of them desired the world's life and its adornment, or stay married to Prophet Muhammad (pbuh) and devote their lives fully for the cause of Islam.

All of them chose the second option and all of them stayed married to Prophet Muhammad (pbuh). After Muhammad (pbuh) passed away, none of them remarried.

FOOTNOTES

1 Narrated by Tirmithi. According to other narrations prophet Muhammad (pbuh) indicated that whoever had one or two or three daughters and he properly looked after them (until they become independent) he would get into God's Paradise.

2 The Qur'an emphasised in many verses that a person must be good to both parents (e.g. Chapter 17, Verse 23).

3 Sahih Abu Dawood. See also The Holy Qur'an (Chapter 2, V 229)

4 Regarding polygamy in other religions, earlier, there were no restrictions even in Hindu religion. It was only in 1954, when the Hindu Marriage Act was passed that it became illegal for a Hindu to have more than one wife. At present, it is the Indian law that restricts a Hindu man from having more than one wife and not the Hindu scriptures.

5 For more details about Jacob family, see Genesis 32:23-24.

6 Muhammad (pbuh) was very sad for the loss of his son to the extent that he cried in front of his companions. Being a father, he couldn't hold his tears. Muhammad told his companions that he would say only what pleases God and a believer should accept God's fate.

7 Please see the Holy Qur'an, Verses 50, 51,52, Chapter 33, regarding the wives of Prophet Muhammad (pbuh).

Human Rights

Freedom, Justice & Protection

"No compulsion" is an essential rule in Islam:
Muhammad proclaimed himself as a Messenger of God. He received a Divine Message to humanity and struggled to convey it to all people but he did not force any one to accept it. He recited the Holy Qur'an which confirms the freedom of belief and freedom choice for all people.

> *"And had your Lord Willed, all people in the earth would have believed (all of them) together. So will you (Muhammad) compel or force people until they become believers?"* The Holy Qur'an, V 99, Ch 10

> *There is no compulsion in religion, truth (the right path) has become distinct from error (wrong path), and whoever rejects evil and believes in God has grasped the most trustworthy hand-hold that never breaks. And God is All-Hearer All-Knower.* The Holy Qur'an, V 256, Ch 2

Morality & equality of all races: In Islam, all people are considered equal under law by reason of their being members of the human race. Piety and excellence of moral character are to be the only criteria for individual superiority in the eyes of God. Muhammad (pbuh) put it in these words:

"Your Lord is One. All humankind are from Adam and Adam was created from dust. An Arab has no superiority over a non-Arab nor does a non-Arab have any superiority over an Arab except by piety (piety motivates good deeds)".[1]

Muhammad encouraged freeing slaves and introduced Islamic regulations to eliminate slavery:

Slavery existed before Muhammad's time. In fact, it was part of many social systems in the world. Slaves were considered as assets and part of people's wealth. Since Islam protects peoples' wealth and property, slavery was gradually abandoned.

Repentance from violations of Islamic rules required releasing slaves or (buying a slave from someone and freeing him or her). As well, abusing or punishing slaves without a just reason required releasing them for repenting of such a sin[2]. This had continued until slavery was fully abolished.

Muhammad (pbuh) encouraged believers to release slaves for the sake of God. On one occasion, Muhammad (pbuh) saw a person called "Abu Mas'ud Al-Badri" hitting and lashing his slave. Muhammad (pbuh) said to him firmly:

"You should know that God is more able and has more power above you than your ability or power above this slave". Abu Mas'ud cooled down and said to Muhammad (pbuh) in an apologetic language: "I will release him for the sake of God". Muhammad (pbuh) said to him: "If you wouldn't do that, the Hellfire will touch your face".

Protection and security of people: Addressing more than 100,000 people, Muhammad (pbuh) said in his last sermon:

"O people, believers are but brothers. No one may take his brother's property without his full consent. Have I delivered the Message? O Allah, my Lord be my witness.

Never go back smiting each other's necks. Verily, I have left among you that which if you take it, you will never stray after me: the Book of God and my example. Have I delivered the Message? O Allah my Lord, be my witness".

All people stand on equal footing in front of the law: Muhammad (pbuh) emphasised that all people should respect the law whereas offenders must be punished regardless of their social status. When the law is applied justly, all people enjoy justice and security.

For example, theft and robbery are an attack on people's properties. Offenders must be punished regardless of their race and social class. Muhammad (pbuh) indicated that no one is above the law even Muhammad's relatives. He stated clearly that he would punish his beloved daughter (Fatima) if she stole (someone's property)[3].

Judge with justice; the story of To'mah and a Jewish man: On one occasion, an Arab man called To'mah Bin Ubayriq stole a metal shield which was part of a suit of armour and hid it at the house of his Jewish friend. The Jewish person was accused of stealing the metal shield but he denied the charge and accused To'mah.

As the offender was not known yet, many Arab Muslims sympathised with To'mah and tried to influence Muhammad's opinion to turn the case against the Jewish man but Islamic justice prevailed, To'mah was proved guilty and the Jewish man was proved to be innocent. In this context, a verse was revealed in the Holy Qur'an asserting justice :

> *"Surely We have sent down to you the Book with truth so that you judge between people according to what God has shown you (taught you justice). So don't be a pleader on behalf of those who betray their trust"*
>
> The Holy Qur'an, V 105, Ch 4

Women's rights and obligations: Muhammad (pbuh) reaffirmed protection of women's rights in his farewell address. He said:

> "O People, it is true that you have certain rights with regard to your women but they also have rights over you.
>
> Remember that you have taken them as your wives only under God's trust and with His permission. Do treat your women well and be kind to them for they are your partners and committed helpers".

Protection of orphans' rights: Muhammad (pbuh) conveyed God's Commandments in relation to orphans. The Holy Qur'an commands for kindness with orphans, fair treatment and protection of their rights.

> *Indeed, those who consume the wealth (property) of the orphans unjustly are only consuming fire into their bellies. For they shall roast in Blaze (burn in Hellfire).*
>
> The Holy Qur'an, Verse 10, Ch 4

Muhammad (pbuh) said:

Looking after orphans

"I and the person who looks after an orphan, will be in Paradise like this" putting his index and middle fingers together" [4].

Deliver the trusts to those entitled to them: Muhammad (pbuh) was asked to lead a funeral prayer for a person, but he first asked his companions: "Did this man borrow any money or has in his possessions any trusts that belong to others?", they said: "Yes". Muhammad (pbuh) asked them first to deliver the trusts to those entitled to them and then he would pray for him. Verse 58, Chapter 4 in the Holy Qur'an states :

> *"Allah Commands you to deliver (render back) trusts (duties) to those entitled to them, and when you judge between people, to judge with justice. How excellent what Allah exhorts (admonishes, cautions) you; surely Allah is All-hearing, All-Seeing".*

Protection of heirs' rights:

According to Islamic law, when someone dies, his or her closest family members are entitled to get stipulated portions of the inheritance (wealth and property of a deceased person). Islam does not allow a person to allocate in the will more than one third of his / her wealth for charity or donation purposes. This is to protect the inheritors' rights and ensure fair distribution of the inheritance among all of them.

Muhammad (pbuh) visited one of his companions after being recovered from an illness. The man said he owned a great wealth and he had only one daughter as an heir (inheritor). He asked Muhammad if he can leave two-thirds of his wealth as a charity. Muhammad said: "No". The man said what about the half. Muhammad said: "No". The man said what about one-third. Muhammad said: "The one-third (agreeing) and the one-third is a lot. To leave your heir(s) wealthy is better than leaving them poor asking for help."

No usury in Islam:

Muhammad (pbuh) said: "God has forbidden you to take usury, therefore all interest obligations shall henceforth be waived. Your capital is yours to keep. You will neither inflict nor suffer any inequity. Allah has judged that there shall be no usury (interest)."

"Those who charge usury are in the same position as those controlled by the devil's influence. This is because they claim that usury is the same as trade. However, God permits trade, and prohibits usury."

The Holy Qur'an, V 275, Ch 2

This is the word "Muhammad" in Arabic being designed in a formative style then repeated in an artistic way. Courtesy of Artist Farid Al-Ali.

Honor killing and bloodshed is forbidden: Muhammad (pbuh) abolished blood vengeance (revenge or retaliation) and vendetta (blood feud or dispute). At his farewell address he declared:

"Every right arising out of homicide (murder) in pre-Islamic days is henceforth waived and the first such right that I waive is that arising from the murder of Rabi'ah (a relative of Muhammad)".

Deliberate murder and killing by mistake: A deliberate murder is subject to retaliation in kind, the killer must be sentenced.

But, whoever kills some one by mistake and causes accidental death must pay compensation to the family of the killed person. At the time of Muhammad, the indemnity was one hundred camels. Muhammad (pbuh) told his people that whoever asks for more than this figure is a person of the Era of Ignorance.

Only fight those who fight you: Muhammad (pbuh) taught his followers to be assertive with their enemies, neither submissive nor aggressive. He was inevitably involved in battle fields. Muhammad (pbuh) set rules and ethics of engagement with enemies in battles and dealing with prisoners of war.

He taught Muslims not to fight civilians and not to attack or kill children or women or elders. He asked them not to destroy the environment or damage trees.

DO NOT KILL

civilians, children, women and elders,

DO NOT DESTROY

environment and do not cut trees

He always reminded them that their involvement in battles should be on assertive ground and for the sake of God Who does not like transgressors. Verse 190, Chapter 2 of the Holy Qur'an sets the basic rule for fighting enemies and aggressors. It clearly states

"And fight for the sake of Allah those who fight you and don't transgress the limits. Verily, Allah does not like transgressors"

Muhammad considered committing suicide a major sin:

Muhammad (pbuh) put it in these words: "Whoever kills him/ herself with a piece of metal, he/she will be resurrected on the Day of Judgment holding the same piece of metal and killing him/herself continuously in the Hellfire forever, and whoever kills him /herself with a poison he/she will be resurrected

Do Not Commit Suicide

holding the same poison and swallowing it continuously in the Hellfire forever, and whoever kills himself/herself by throwing himself/herself from a high place such as a mountain, he or she will do the same in the Hellfire forever".[5]

Sanctity & inviolability of human lives:

Because God is the creator of life and the only controller of it, He owns every creature's life. God states in the Holy Qur'an in relation to the first murder incident in the history when Cain, the son of Adam, killed his brother Abel:

> "For that We decreed for the Children of Israel that whosoever murders a human-being who had not committed murder or horrendous crimes (mischief on the earth), it shall be as if he had murdered all the people, and whosoever saves the life of a human-being, it shall be as if he had saved the life of all mankind".
>
> The Holy Qur'an, V 32, Ch 5

No Violence

Muhammad condemned violence: Muhammad (pbuh) never used violence as a tool to convey God's Message or impose God's religion. Although he established an Islamic state in Madinah, he never used the small Muslim community who remained in Mecca to create trouble or assassinate his enemies. In fact, he asked his followers to respect the social order of the society they lived in.

Muhammad (pbuh) taught believers that whenever and wherever gentleness or kindness is used in a matter, it will add value to it and will bring good results. He also taught that roughness and indelicate behaviours will spoil every matter.

> *"O mankind!*
> *We have created you from a male and a female, and have*
> *made you nations and tribes that you may know one*
> *another. Verily the most honorable of you in the sight of*
> *Allah, is the best in conduct and most pious. Verily Allah*
> *is All-Knower, All-Aware".*
>
> The Holy Qur'an, V 13, Ch 49. The Inner Apartments (Al-Hujurát)

Human rights are rights inherent to all human beings
regardless of their race, sex, color, language, religion
and social status.
People are born free and equal in dignity and rights.
They should act towards one another in a spirit of
brotherhood.

FOOTNOTES

1 Riyadh Al-Salihin (1604/5)

2 Riyadh Al-Salihin (1603/4), (1605/6)

3 For more information about Islamic law and justice in Islam please see http://www.islamreligion.com/category/110/

4 Sahih Al-Bukhari (34/8)

5 Sahih Al-Bukhari (5778) and Sahih Muslim (109)

Nelson Mandela the first president of democratic South Africa. He represents the struggle for a demorcratic and free South Africa in which all people live together as one nation united in their diversity.

Artistic designs from the word "Muhammad" in Arabic. Courtesy of Farid Al-Ali.

Environment

The bowing tree: It was found in a camping site in Nowra, South of Sydney, Australia. It resembles bowing to God in the Muslim's prayers. The lower edge of the tree looks like the head of a bowing person.

Muhammad's Teachings to Preserve the Environment

Environment

Muhammad called for a green world:

He linked the preservation of the environment to the belief in God Who created all beings. Therefore, a believer in God can not cause mischief to the environment because it is part of God's Kingdom. Harming the environment and wasting or polluting its resources (water, plants, animals, soil, air, marine ecosystem, etc) is not acceptable from an Islamic point of view.

"Any Muslim who plants a seed that grows to a level, people or animals or birds can benefit or eat from it, then this act is considered as a Sadaqa" (a charity that is rewarded by God).[1]

Muhammad (Pbuh)

Natural resources are in perfect equilibrium:

Muhammad (pbuh) taught his followers that all natural resources were created by God and were set by Him in perfect equilibrium. God said in the Holy Qur'an which was revealed to Muhammad (pbuh)

> "Verily all things We created are in proportion and measure".
>
> "... and everything with Him is in due proportion (measured)".
>
> "...the work (creation & artistry of Allah) Who perfected all things (disposed all things in perfect order)"
>
> The Holy Qur'an, V 49, Ch 54; V 8, Ch 13; V 88, Ch 27.

People have equal rights in natural resources: Natural resources are the gift of God to all mankind. They should not be wasted or monopolized. Muhammad (pbuh) stated that people have equal shares in water, grass (green cover) and fire (energy)[2] (except what was officialy privatized).

"Blessed be Allah the best of creators"
Fauna and flora are the creation of God

"No Harm" is a general rule: Muhammad (pbuh) set a general rule for protecting the natural resources, preserving the environment and securing people when he said to his companions:

"You are not to harm or to be harmed".³

"Faith (in God) can be branched into more than 70 parts topped by testifying the oneness of God. The last part is removing harm from people's way". ⁴

Muhammad (Pbuh)

This is the word "Muhammad" written in a formative style of Arabic calligraphy. It looks like green leaves from a tree.

Environment

Muhammad emphasised water rationing and condemned wasting and overspending:

Muhammad (pbuh) stated clearly to a companion (who was performing ablution) not to waste water even if he were close to a running river[5].

On another occasion Muhammad (pbuh) told his companions not to pollute stagnant water or urinate in it[6].

God said in the Holy Qur'an:

> *"...Out of water, We made every living creature."*
>
> *"Verily the spendthrifts (wasteful people) are the brothers of devils and the Satan has ever been ungrateful to his Lord."*
>
> *"...Eat and drink with no extravagance. Certainly He does not like the prodigals (those who waste and overspend)."*
>
> The Holy Qur'an V30, Ch 21; V27, Ch 17; V31, Ch 7

Add value to the environment: Muhammad (pbuh) encouraged people to continuously add value to the environment even if the whole universe is collapsing and life is ending on this planet. He said:

"If the Hour came (i.e. the end of the worldly life) and someone had a seedling in his hand and he were able to plant it, then let him do it"[7]. Believers in God are required to add value to the environment and protect it. God does not like those who cause mischief (on the earth) and destroy the crops and cattle[8].

Add Value

"And seek the dwelling of the Hereafter and don't forget your portion of lawful enjoyment in this world and do good as Allah has been good to you and seek no mischief in the land, Verily Allah does not like those who cause mischief"

The Holy Qur'an V 77, Ch 28

Muhammad (pbuh) called for ethical treatment of animals: He was against detaining or confining or restraining animals for no genuine reason. Also, he didn't like lashing animals or hitting them on their faces. He used different teaching

styles to emphasise the good treatment of animals. (e.g. direct instructive style, indirect style through story telling and practical teaching by taking action in real cases).

Animals and all creatures form part of communities like us: Muhammad (pbuh) conveyed God's Words in this context. God said in the Holy Qur'an:

"There is not an animal or creature (that lives and moves) on the earth, nor a being that flies on its wings, but they are communities like you. We have not neglected anything in the Book and they (all creation) shall be gathered to their Lord in the end".

The Holy Qur'an, V 38, Ch 6, The Cattle

Ethical Treatment of Animals

On one occasion, Muhammad (pbuh) wanted to pass a message to a person regarding good treatment of animals. He told him that his camel "complained" to him because it was loaded with more than it could bear.

On another occasion, Muhammad (pbuh) said to his companions: "Whoever captured the babies of this bird should return them back to their mother (which was running like a headless chick).[9]

Muhammad taught clemency with animals in action: In the year 627 CE he was leading his followers and heading to Mecca to perform Umrah (i.e. religious rites and worship). Muhammad (pbuh) changed the route of the whole convoy because he did not want to frighten a female dog who was giving birth in a spot blocking their way. That spot was close to an area called "Hudaybiya" (which is still known by this name until now in Saudi Arabia).

Halal Meat

Halal means more than Halal food: Muhammad (pbuh) taught his followers that they have no right to kill any animal unless permitted by God. It is only with God's permission (to whom all creatures belong to) that certain types of animals can be slaughtered for human consumption. Only vegetarian animals can be slaughtered to be eaten with the exception of pigs (e.g. cows, sheep, chicken and birds that eat no flesh).

Muhammad (pbuh) taught his followers that lawful (Halal) killing of animals should be done in the least painful manner: For example, the animal can't be slaughtered by a blunt blade (it must be very sharp). An animal must not be hit by a stone or slaughtered next to another animal watching the slaughter process. Muhammad (pbuh) said to a person who was slaughtering an animal besides another one "do you want to kill the other animal twice?[10]

You will be rewarded for being kind to animals: A kind act, even to animals, deserves to be rewarded by God. Muhammad (pbuh) once told his companions a story of a thirsty man who found a well of water and went down to drink. When he went up, he found a thirsty dog (gasping) so he went down in the well again to fill his shoe with water and bring it up to the dog. God was thankful for this man and he forgave his past sins.

On another occasion, Muhammad (pbuh) told his companions that God had punished a woman because she imprisoned or confined a cat until it died. She neither fed the cat nor let it go.[11]

"There is not an animal or creature (that lives and moves) on the earth, nor a being that flies on its wings, but they are communities like you.

The Holy Qur'an, V 38, Ch 6, The Cattle

FOOTNOTES

1   Narrated by Bukhari (2320) and Muslim (1552) and
    Riyadh Al-Saliheen (135/19)
2   Narrated by Imam Ahmad and Abu Dawood
3   Narrated by Nawawi, Mazini - Muwatta
4   Narrated in Riyadh Al-Saliheen (125/9)
5   Narrated by Imam Ahmad and Ibn Maja
6   Narrated by Nassa'i, Imam Ahmad and Ibn Maja
7   Narrated by Bukhari
8   The Qur'an (Ch 2, V 205)
9   Riyadh Al-Saliheen (2/1610)
10 Narrated in Riyadh Al-Saliheen
11 Narrated in Riyadh Al-Saliheen

The Miracle

"Say, O people,
I am the messenger of Allah (God) to
all of you
To Him belongs the sovereignty of the
heavens and the earth
There is no god except He (Allah)
He controls life and death
So believe in Allah and His Messenger,
the illiterate prophet; who believes in
Allah and His Words:
Follow him, that you may be guided"

The Holy Qur'an V158, Ch 7 (The Heights)

God's Miracle to Muhammad

Many scholars believe that Muhammad's mission to convey God's Message and bring people to faith was harder than the mission of many messengers and prophets before him. The main miracle he brought was the Qur'an which was recited in original Arabic as a divine revelation from God.

Despite the resistance he received from his own people who spoke Arabic, he conveyed Islam to nations and communities of different languages, cultures and religions outside the Arabian Peninsula.

> "Will they not ponder on the Qur'an? If it had been from other than Allah they would have found therein much incongruity (inconsistency)".
>
> The Holy Qur'an, V 82, Ch 4

Why is the Holy Qur'an considered an eternal miracle?

Unlike physical miracles that were brought by true prophets and messengers and seen only by the people who lived at their times, the Holy Qur'an is considered by Muslims as an eternal miracle that can be touched, seen, read and conveyed from one generation to another.

Muslims consider the Holy Qur'an as Gods' Word and His eternal Message to all mankind. They believe it is the only book that contains the Words of God without being rephrased by His Messenger or anyone else. Verse 88, Chapter 17 states:

> "Say (O'Muhammad): "If the whole humanity and Jinns were to gather together to produce the like of this Qur'an they could not produce the like thereof even if they backed up each other with help and support".
>
> The Holy Qur'an V88, Ch 17

Incomparable preservation of the Quranic text: The present Holy Qur'an is identical to the one revealed to Prophet Muhammad (pbuh) more than fourteen centuries ago. Initially, it was memorized by most pious Muslims (word by word and letter by letter).

Then, soon after the passing away of Muhammad (pbuh), the complete Holy Qur'an was first compiled in one book when Abu Baker As-Siddiq became the first caliph in Islam. Several genuine copies were generated and distributed to different Islamic states or regions when Othman Bin Affan became the third caliph 13 years after the passing away of Prophet Muhammad (pbuh).

This is part of a verse in the Holy Qura'n. God says to His people: "Call Me and I will answer you". V 60, Ch 40 (The Forgiver)

The concept of recurrence "Tawaator" confirms the absolute authenticity of Qur'an because it indicates that the same text was narrated by different groups of people and passed from one generation to another without contradictions or discrepancies or discontinuity.

Distinctiveness of Qur'an: It should be noticed that Muhammad's sayings and teachings were not mixed with the Holy Qur'an (which only contains God's Words without any human comments or elaborations). Muhammad's sayings and teachings were collected in books which were called "The Sunnah or Hadith of the Prophet". They include his teachings, his way of life and explanation of the Book (The Holy Qur'an).

Comparison between Hadith books and other holy books: Most holy books of different religions are authored and written by human beings with their own words and phrases.

Since Hadith books were collected by Muslim scholars and contained Muhammad's own sayings and teachings, many researchers consider them as similar to other holy books.

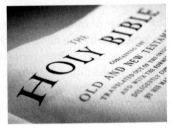

For example, the Bible was written over a period of 1400 to 1800 years by 40 different authors. It is a compilation of 66 separate books, divided into two primary divisions: the Old Testament (containing 39 books) and the New Testament (containing 27 books).

> The language of the Holy Qur'an indicates that God is speaking to humanity. It frequently uses the pronoun "We" with verbs and the word "Say" (i.e. Say O Muhammad to them). Muhammad (pbuh) stated clearly that what he recited as Qur'an is God's Own Words not his words.

Incomparable preservation of the style of reciting Qur'an: When the Holy Qur'an is read or recited, the term "Tajweed" is commonly mentioned or highlighted to describe the knowledge that deals with the rules controlling the way of reading the Holy Qur'an.

Muslims trust it is not only the Quranic text that was uniquely preserved but also the styles in which Muhammad (pbuh) and his companions recited it.

The styles of reciting the Holy Qur'an are documented by the names of the narrators and reciters starting from those who heard it from Muhammad (pbuh) until now. This is across the whole Islamic world and continued from one generation to another generation until now.

Tajweed a Unique Science

It is believed that "Tajweed" is a very unique science not available in other religions. It reflects the highest level of attention given by the companions of Muhammad (pbuh) in order to preserve the way he recited the Holy Qur'an word by word.

The rich language of the Holy Qur'an: It was revealed in original Arabic. Muslim scholars believe that Arabic language is superior to many other languages as it is well supported by a huge number of words and a strong Arabic grammar.

This indicates that the Arabic language can be more precise than other languages in describing God's Words. For example, Arabic language has 28 letters, some of them don't exist in other languages such as "Dhad" which is the heavy "D" and "Tau" which is a heavy "T".

The number of derivations from each original or root word can exceed 100 derivations and accordingly the total number of words in Arabic language may exceed **six million words.** This is far higher than the number of words of most known languages in the world.

Significant Scientific Facts in the Qur'an

The big bang and the creation of the universe:

At Muhammad's time (pbuh) nobody knew anything about the creation of the universe and the motion of the planets

and whether the earth was flat or round. Muslims believe that God the Creator of the universe is the only One Who knows how it was created.

Fourteen centuries ago, the Holy Qur'an mentioned (in a miraculous manner) the creation of the universe, the motion of the sun and the motion of the moon, the rotation of the earth and the formation of day and night.

Modern science explains the creation of the universe by the "Big Bang theory" which is supported by observational and experimental data gathered over decades. According to the "Big Bang theory" the whole universe was initially one big mass then there was a huge explosion which resulted in the

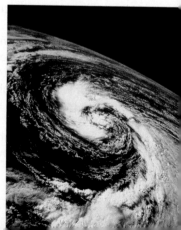

formation of galaxies out of agglomerated clouds of celestial matter in a smoke or gaseous form.

The expansion of the universe:

In 1925, American astronomer Edwin Hubble provided observational evidence that stars are moving away from each other which implies that galaxies and the whole universe is expanding. Also, it is an established scientific fact that planets move in elliptical orbits around the sun and rotate around their axes.

One will be surprised at the similarities between the modern scientific discoveries and the following verses in the Holy Qur'an which were recited by Muhammad (pbuh) more that 14 centuries ago and preserved until now.

...t the disbelievers known that the heaven and the earth were joined together as one piece and We separated them apart and We made every living thing of water? Will they not then believe? V 30, Ch 21 (Prophets)

He, "the Almighty God", turned to the heaven when it was smoke and said to it and to the earth: come together willingly or unwillingly, they said: we come together in willing obedience V 11, Ch 41 (Fussilat)

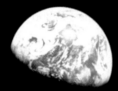

"And it is He Who created the night and the day, and the sun and the moon. All (the celestial bodies) swim along (float), each in its rounded course (orbit)".
V 33, Ch 21 (Prophets)

"With power and skill We created the heaven and We are continuously expanding it." V47, Ch 51 (Thariyat).

Embryology and creation of humankind: Muhammad (pbuh) recited the following miraculous verse that explains the creation of mankind. Such knowledge was not known at his time and the science of embryology was not yet discovered 1400 years ago.

> *"...He creates you in the wombs of your mothers, creation after creation, in a three veils of darkness (threefold gloom). This is Allah, your Lord. The Sovereignty is His. There is no God except Him. How then are you turned away?".*
>
> The Holy Qur'an, V 6, Ch 39 (Al-Zomar)

Modern science explains that there are three layers that form veils of darkness that surround the fetus in the womb and provide sturdy and powerful protection for the embryo; (1) the interior abdominal wall of the mother, (2) the uterine wall and (3) the amino-chorionic membrane.

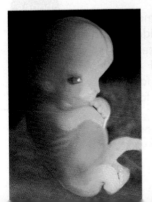

The Miracle

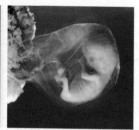

The creation of humankind is described miraculously in the following verse from the Holy Qur'an

sperm

⬇

blood clot

⬇

fetus lump

⬇

bones

⬇

flesh

"*Verily We created man from clay (quintessence of product of wet earth), then We placed him as a drop (of sperm) in a safe lodging; Then We made the sperm into a clot of congealed (solid) blood, then of that clot We made a fetus lump, then We made out of that lump bones then covered the bones with flesh, and then produced it another creation*".

The Holy Qur'an, V 12-14, Ch 23

Surprisingly, embryo development as stated in the Holy Qur'an was found identical to the discoveries of medicine science. Also, it was

found that bones were formed before the formation of flesh, exactly as mentioned in the above verse. [2]

In addition, scientists discovered that the hearing sense for the embryo develops in the mothers' womb before the sense of sight. This is compatible to the sequence mentioned in the Holy Qur'an. Verses 9:32, 2:76, 78:23 all refer to the hearing sense before the sight sense.

> "...So blessed be Allah the best of Creators".
> The Holy Qur'an, V14, Ch 23 (The believers)

309 Astonishing counting of years: Verse 25, Chapter 18 (The Cave) in the Holy Qur'an talks about the seven sleepers and states that they spent 300 years in the cave and additional "9 years". Nobody knew at Muhammad's time why the verse didn't state the total number as "309 years" instead of the above expression.

Also, in Arabia, nobody knew at that time the difference between lunar year and Solar / Gregorian calendar. The Lunar year is 11 days shorter than the Solar one. The amazing fact is: in 300 years, the difference between the lunar year and Solar/Gregorian year is **9** years.

The Holy Qur'an is commonly printed in 604 pages. It contains 80000 words approximately which form 6348 verses that comprise 114 chapters. The longest chapter in the Holy Qur'an is composed of 286 verses and the shortest one is composed of 3 verses only.

Amazing information of future events:
Verses 2-5, Chapter 30 in the Holy Qur'an state:

*"The Romans have been defeated at the nearest/
lowest land but they will gain victory within a
few years. Allah has the Command in the former case
and in the latter and on that day believers (in God) will
rejoice and will be pleased with the victory of God. He
helps to victory whom He Wills. He is the All Mighty, the
Merciful".*

At Muhammad's time (Pbuh), it is virtually impossible for Arabs to predict how the development of the conflict would be between the two superpowers (at their time) within the next ten years and whether a defeated empire can restore victory within few years. It is a historical fact that the Persian Empire defeated the Roman Empire in the period (614-619 CE) in Palestine area and captured Jerusalem. But within a few years, the Romans had restored victory over the Persians at Nineveh (a city in Iraq).

Incredible geography:
Surprisingly, the recent geological research found that the Dead Sea which lies in the Jordan rift valley is the deepest hyper saline lake in the world. It is 422 meters (1,385 ft) below the sea level. Its shores are the lowest point on the surface of earth. The above Qur'anic verses indicate that the Romans were defeated at the nearest Roman land to Arabia and in fact it included the lowest land on the earth.

Note: The original Arabic word "adna" (verse 3 above) indicates both meanings, nearest and lowest

FOOTNOTES

1. The Old Testament was written in Hebrew 1500-400 BC. New Testament was composed in Greek and written during the second half of the first century AD. It is generally agreed that the Book of Matthew was the first Gospel written between A.D. 50 and 75. Of the four Gospel's, John's is considered to have been the last one written, around A.D. 85.

2. See more information about embryology
   www.quranandscience.com
   www.islamreligion.com

3. To access more information about the scientific facts in the Holy Qur'an you can browse www.eajaz.org

This is a testimony in Arabic calligraphy which was designed in an artistic way. It states: I witness that there is no God except Allah and Muhammad is His servant and His messenger.

His Sayings

Muhammad's sayings and teachings are very influential as they covered most aspects of life. They emanated from a base of wisdom and Divine revelation.
His sayings, actions, approvals and attributes better known as "sunnah" represent the second source of Islamic legislation after The Holy Qur'an.

Your companion (i.e. Muhammad) has not strayed from the path of truth nor has he been deluded. Nor does he speak out of whim

The Holy Quran, V 2,3, Ch 53

Muhammad said (interlacing his both hands fingers):

"Believers are a structure like, they fasten each other"

Narrated by Bukhari, Muslim & Tirmithi

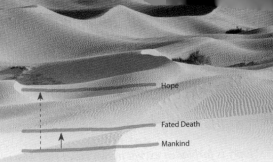

Hope

Fated Death

Mankind

Muhammad (pbuh) drew three lines on the sand and said:
"This is the human being (who has many hopes and plans
in this worldly life). While he lives to attain or accomplish
these hopes death comes to him".

(Narrated by Bukhari, Turmithi)

"Avail five before five :
  Your youth before senility (old age)
  Fitness before sickness
  Wealth before poverty (needy)
  Free time before busy time
  Life before death". (Riyadh Saliheen)

"The perfect believers are those who have the best manners".
(Narrated by Turmithi)

"Two graces, many people underestimate; health and free (leisure) time". (Riyadh Saliheen)

"Envy is forbidden except in two cases (you wish to have the same thing others have but no bad wishes to them). The first one is a man, God bestowed on him wealth, so he spends it righteously, the second case is a man, God bestowed on him wisdom, so he acts according to it and teaches it to others". (Bukhari, 73/15)

"Make things easy to people (concerning religious matters), and do not make it hard for them; give them good tidings and do not make them run away".

(Bukhari, 69/11)

"Those who do honest trading and business based on clear terms, God blesses them and their business (trade). Contrary, God does not bless those who lie and hide facts".

(Bukhari, 2082/22)

"You will not be a believer in God unless you like for your brethrens what you like for yourself". *(Bukhari, 13/7)*

"Every Muslim should pay Sadaqa (spend for charity), if he didn't find what to spend then let him work in order to benefit himself and be able to pay charity, if he didn't find a job, then let him help others (this is an act of charity), if he didn't find anyone to help, let him do good deeds and refrain from (avoid) doing bad or evil deeds. This is a charity for him". *(Bukhari, 1445/30)*

"When man dies, he gains no rewards except from three things; in case he had dedicated a charity that people can continuously profit from or he had left knowledge or a science that benefits the humanity or if he had left a good (faithful) son who keeps on praying and asking Gods blessings and forgiveness to his parents".

(this is applicable for both males and females)

(Narrated by Muslim, Tirmithi, Nassa'i)

MUHAMMAD

"Fear Allah wherever you are, ensure (follow) a bad deed with a good deed as it erases it, and deal with people with high ethics". (Tirmithi - 1987 & Ahmad 5/153)

"Goodness (rightness) is good morality; and sin (misdeed) is what embarrasses you (i.e. you are not comfortable within yourself) and you hate it to be known by others". (Muslim, 15/2553)

"A strong person is not the one who throws his adversaries to the ground. A strong person is he who contains himself when he is angry".

(Narrated by Bukhari, Muslim & Ahmad)

"Whoever believes in Allah and the Day of judgement should say good (words) or keep silent and whoever believes in Allah and the Day of judgment must honor (be generous with) his neighbor and whoever believes in Allah and the Day of judgment must honor (be generous with) his guest".

(Bukhari, 6018 & Muslim 74-47)

(Please note all the above sayings are applicable for both males and females)

MUHAMMAD

Sayings of Prophet Muhammad in Relation to Food and Medicine

Prevention is better than cure

Although Muhammad (pbuh) was not a physician, his sayings in relation to food, healthy eating habits, treatment with herbs and alternative medicine were collected in books later known as "The Prophetic Medicine".

Muhammad (pbuh) indicated on several occasions the belly is the worst pot to fill. Small meals and a few bites that satisfy hunger will be better than filling the stomach. It will help a great deal avoid health complications.

The Belly, the Worst Thing to Fill

He encouraged his companions to eat and drink in moderation, avoid obesity and maintain an active and a healthy style of life. He recited God's Words in this context. Verse 31, Chapter 7 in the Holy Qur'an states:

> *"O Children of Adam! Wear your beautiful apparel at every time and place of prayer: eat and drink: but do not be prodigal (waste by excess). He (God) does not like prodigals (extravagant people)."*

Muhammad prescribing barley: Today, there is a great deal of research that demonstrates the amazing health benefits of barley. Barley grass is a whole food supplement.

It contains a wide spectrum of enzymes, vitamins, minerals, phytochemicals and all eight essential amino acids including Tryptophan which helps prevent depression.

Barley as an Anti-depressant

Muhammad (pbuh) recommended barley soup (talbinah) for stomach disorder and indicated in his undisputable sayings that it helps relieve sorrow and depression. His wife Aisha used to recommend the close relatives of a deceased person to have Talbina soup in order to relief sorrow. (Narrated in Sahih Bukhari).

According to medical research, depressive illness is found to be caused by a decrease of certain chemicals or neurotransmitters in the brain that are responsible for mood. Antidepressants stimulate chemical changes that increase the levels of these neurotransmitters.

The three main neurotransmitters associated with mood are serotonin, norepinephrine and dopamine. Barley was found to influence serotonin in a positive way that relieves depression. The prescription of Barley by Muhammad (pbuh) 1400 years ago was definitely a miraculous medicine.

Wheat or Barley?

It is revealing that Muhammad (pbuh) did not indulge in regular wheat consumption, but ate instead mostly barley and bread made from barley flour.

It is discovered that whole grain barley has many health benefits. It can regulate blood sugar, prevent tiny blood clots, and reduce the body's production of cholesterol.

It is part of Muhammad's teachings to have small meals during the day. Should some one likes to eat more, the belly must not be more than two thirds full. He told his companions to keep one third of their stomach's space for food and one third for drink and the last third should be kept empty for breath.

(Tirmithi - Miqdam Bin Ma'd Yakrib)

1/3 Food
+
1/3 Drink
+
1/3 Empty

Zamzam mineral water: Zamzam is the name of mineral water that comes out of a well 20 meters east of Kaaba in Makkah city the holiest place in Islam. Muslims believe that it was miraculously generated thousands of years ago when Ibrahim's son Ishmael was thirsty and kept crying and kicking the ground until water gushed out (He was with his mother Hagar).

It is slightly alkaline (pH=7.5) and has a distinct taste. *(Please note that drinking de-mineralized water such as distilled waters will create an acid pH in the stomach and intestines. Also, it will aggravate acid reflux).*

Muhammad (pbuh) said that Zamzam water is a blessed water from God. It is a lavish meal and a healer from many diseases, (narrated by Bazzar and Tabarani).

Mineral water is classified by the U.S. FDA or Food and Drug Authority as having at least 250 parts per million (ppm) (total dissolved solids TDS).

Chemical analysis of Zamzam water revealed that it has TDS in excess of 1000 ppm of mg/L. It complies with World Health Organization (WHO) standards for potable water.

It is a plentiful meal that contains a range of minerals that the human body needs such as calcium (which is needed for strong bones and for the heart, muscles and nerves to function properly), Fluoride which is necessary for teeth and bicarbonates which helps food digestion.

Zamzam water is one of the richest potable waters in Calcium. It has 195-200 mg/L Calcium. (this is about 20% of the average recommended daily intake of calcium for adults).

It is higher than many known mineral waters on the earth such as "Evian" (78-80 mg/L Calcium) and "Perrier" (147-150 mg/L Calcium)[5].

Mineral water has a wide range of therapeutic functions that can relieve and treat muscle and joint inflammation, rheumatism and arthritis.

This is the word "Rasul Allah"(Messenger of God) in Arabic being written in a formative style which looks like a droplet of water. Courtesy of Farid Al-Ali

Truffle as a medicine:

Muhammad (pbuh) said: "Truffles are a kind of 'Manna' (sent down upon the children of Israel) and their juice is a medicine for the eyes".
Narrated by Bukhari, Muslim & Tirmithi

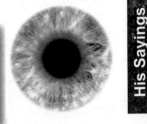

Truffle is a fleshy fungus mushroom-like plant that belongs to the Agaricaceae family. It grows in groups under the surface of the soil (2-50 cm deep) in desert moist areas without leaves or roots. It has a distinct smell and can be white, gray or brown in color.

According to the analytical research, 77% of truffle is water and the remaining part is a mix of protein, fat, carbohydrates and other materials.

However, modern science discoveries indicate that the liquid of truffles has an effective curable effect for many eye diseases including Trachoma which is an infectious eye disease that causes damage to the cornea cells.

Muhammad and olive oil:

Muhammad (pbuh) described olive oil as it comes from a blessed tree. He recommended his companions to eat olive oil and to anoint or smear it over their body skin (Narrated by Tirmithi)

All modern scientific discoveries confirm that olive oil is full of health benefits. Most of the fatty acid "building blocks" that make up olive oil come from mono-unsaturated fat (good fat) which offers protection against heart disease by controlling LDL (bad cholesterol) cholesterol levels while raising HDL (the good cholesterol) levels.

Olive oil is very well tolerated by the stomach. Its protective function has a beneficial effect for treating ulcers and gastritis.

Extra virgin olive oil, from the first pressing of the olives, contains higher levels of antioxidants, particularly vitamin E and phenols, because it is less processed.

Today, olive oil is considered a good remedy for skin problems and an effective moisturizer.

Those at risk for diabetes are advised to combine a low-fat, high-carbohydrate diet with olive oil. Studies show this combination is superior at controlling blood sugar levels compared to a diet that consists entirely of low-fat meals.

Prophet Muhammad (pbuh) said:

"Eat olive oil and smear it over your bodies"

(Narrated by Tirmithi)

The story of Suraqah; a prediction takes place 20 years later:

When Muhammad (pbuh) migrated to Madinah with his close companion Abu Bakr (622 CE), the Meccan leaders announced a large reward of 100 camels for anyone who could bring Muhammad (pbuh) dead or alive.

Unfortunately Muhammad (pbuh) and his companion were tracked down by one of the Arab knights named Suraqah bin Malik who was tempted by the big reward. On the way his horse stumbled and he fell on the ground few times. He considered these unusual incidents as an indirect message that Muhammad (pbuh) probably had been supported by divine power.

When Suraqah approached Muhammad (pbuh), Muhammad said to him:" Do return to your people and I promise you that one day (under the umbrella of the Islamic state) you would wear the bangles (bracelets) of Chosroes (the Persian ruler). Suraqah asked in wonderment if Muhammad (pbuh) meant the bangles of Khusrow bin Hormuz, **the emperor of Iran**. Muhammad (pbuh) said yes with full confidence and strong faith that the religion of Islam will reach Persia and will be known all over the world.

Suraqah returned back to Makkah but he didn't embrace Islam until Muhammad (pbuh) took over Makkah peacefully 8 years later (year 630 CE).

Muhammad (pbuh) passed away in the year 632 CE and his promise to Suraqah was believed by his companions as genuine and would happen one day.

Time passed until Omar Bin Al-Khattab became the second caliph (ruler of the Muslim state). At his time, Islam reached Persia in the year 642 CE and all the treasures of Khusrow, the emperor of Persia fell in the hands of Omar.

Omar remembered the story of Suraqah and asked his companions to bring him in. (20 years passed since this story took place and Suraqah had become an old man).

After prayer congregation, Omar said to Suraqah: *"Here are the bangles of Khusrow, the emperor of Persia, this is what Muhammad (pbuh) had promised you. Put them on and let*

all Muslims see them so everyone becomes certain that Muhammad's promise is fulfilled."

Suraqah cried and every one wept. Muhammad's prediction became a reality 10 years after he passed away.

Epilogue

Prophet Muhammad (pbuh) Mosque
(Al-Masjid AL-Nabawi) Madinah, Saudi Arabia

Note: The house and the tomb of prophet
Muhammad (pbuh) were joined to the mosque.

Muhammad.. The Man

History has recorded Muhammad's sublime and humane dealing with people. His call and teachings were based on amicability and fraternity. Adversity had no place in his conduct.

Michael Hart stated in his book "The 100; A Ranking of the Most Influential Persons in History":

"Of humble origins, Muhammad founded and promulgated one of the world's great religions and became an immensely effective political leader. Today, thirteen centuries after his death, his influence is still powerful and pervasive. The majority of persons in this book, had the advantage of being born and raised in centers of civilisation, highly cultured and politically pivotal nations".

"It is this unparalleled combination of secular and religious influence which I feel entitles Muhammad to be considered the most influential single figure in human history".

Michael Hart

Muhammad however was born in the year 570 CE, in the city of Mecca, in southern

 This is the word "Muhammad" in Arabic being designed in a formative style.

Arabia, at that time a backward area of the world, far from the centers of trade, art and learning".

"It is probable that the relative influence of Muhammad on Islam has been larger than the combined influence of Jesus Christ and St. Paul on Christianity. On the purely religious level, then it seems likely that Muhammad has been as influential in human history as Jesus".

Muhammad, the leader:

Speaking objectively about Muhammad, the French writer and politician Alphonse de Lamartine wrote in his book Histoire de la Turquie:

"If the grandeur of the aim, the smallness of the means, the immensity of the result are the three measures of a man's genius, who would dare humanly compare a great man of modern history with Muhammad?".

"Never has a man proposed for himself, voluntarily or involuntarily, a goal more sublime, since this goal was beyond measure: undermine the superstitions placed between the creature and the Creator, give back God to man and man to God, reinstate the rational and saintly idea of

divinity in the midst of this prevailing chaos of material and disfigured gods of idolatry. Never has a man accomplished in such a short time such an immense and long lasting revolution in the world".

Lamartine also indicated that Muhammad didn't move weapons and empires to create a material power but he moved ideas, beliefs, and souls. He founded upon a Book; of which each letter has become a law; a spiritual nationality embracing people of all languages and races in the world.

Muhammad, the Messenger of God:

In the year 630 CE, Muhammad (pbuh) gained victory over the Meccan chiefs and entered Mecca peacefully. He returned home not to live there for the rest of his life but to clear paganism and liberate or restore the original purpose of Ka'ba (the cubical building that was established by Prophet Abraham to worship one God). He removed all idols from around the Ka'ba and asked his companion Bilal to climb on top of the Ka'ba and call:

God is Greatest, God is Greatest, I witness that there is no deity but Allah and I witness that Muhammad is His messenger.

Muhammad wanted the key for the door of Ka'ba so he called Othman Bin Talha (of Bani-Shayba family) who was the keeper of the Ka'ba key. It is important to know that there was a treaty before Islam in which the honour of being a custodian or a warden of the Ka'ba was given to the family of Bani Shayba. This honour and responsibility was passed from the grandfathers to the sons in the same family until it reached Othman Bin Talha.

Othman Bin Talha was a new muslim at that time. Many years ago he refused to let Muhammad (pbuh) even enter the Ka'ba and pray inside it like other people since he did not believe him. When Muhammad (pbuh) returned to Mecca, Othman had no choice but to give him the key and lose the honour of keeping it.

At that moment many people asked Muhammad (pbuh) to grant them the honour of keeping the key of Ka'ba and thousands of Muslims were looking at Muhammad (pbuh) to see who would be the new custodian of the Ka'ba key.

Breaking a moment of silence, Muhammad (pbuh) opened the door of Ka'ba and cleared it of idols. He looked at Othman Bin Talha and said to him (respecting previous agreements):

"Today is a day of loyalty and piety! Take the key back. As from now and until the Day of Judgment, no one can take it from you (family of Bani Shayba) unless he was an aggressor".

A moment of fidelity that had lasted until now: You may be surprised to know that the key is still being held by the offspring of Bani Shayba family until NOW!

More than 1400 years passed and the key is still given from one generation of the Bani Shayba family to the next generation. Until now, no one dares to take it from them otherwise he or she would be considered as an "aggressor" according to Muhammad's description.

Nowadays, when the Saudi authorities perform their annual cleaning and preparation of Ka'ba for the annual pilgrimage, they contact a person from the Bani Shayba family (who is currently a Saudi family) to open the Ka'ba door for them.

Karen Armstrong the author of "Muhammad a Prophet for Our Time" indicated that we must approach the life of Prophet Muhammad in a balanced way in order to appreciate his considerable achievements. He had important lessons, not only for Muslims, but also for Western people.

Muhammad literally sweated with the effort to bring peace to war-torn Arabia. His life was a tireless campaign against greed, injustice, and arrogance.

Karen trusts that If we are to avoid catastrophe, the Muslim and Western Worlds must learn not merely to tolerate but to appreciate one another. A good place to start is with the figure of Muhammad.

Gold plated door from Prophet Muhammad (pbuh) Mosque
(Al-Masjid Al-Nabawi), Madinah, Saudi Arabia

The Sacred Mosque (Al Masjid Al-Haram) in Makkah – Saudi Arabia. This is the holiest Mosque in Islam (and the whole world). The black building is the Kaaba. Muslims believe God Commanded Prophet Abraham to erect or establish the Kaaba to glorify and worship Him (The One God). When Muslims pray to God, they direct their faces (from all over the world) toward the Kaaba.

Prophet Muhammad (pbuh) indicated that praying in the Sacred Mosque is highly rewardable. One prayer in the Sacred Mosque is equivalent to 100,000 prayers.

Chapter 12

Islamic
Art, Calligraphy and Architecture

Photo taken by Peter Gould. Sultan Qaboos Grand Mosque - Oman

Islamic art and calligraphy, Bahrain ▲

Digital Artist Peter Gould

Sydney-born designer & digital artist Peter Gould founded Azaan (www.azaan.com.au) to explore his passion for contemporary graphic design, art, photography and the rich visual & spiritual traditions of Islam. His travels and studies throughout the Muslim world have inspired a unique cultural fusion that is reactive to a world of misunderstanding. Peter's work has reached many audiences locally and abroad through exhibitions and collaborations with other artists.

Farid Al-Ali, Plastic Artist and Calligrapher, Kuwait

He is the director of Kuwait Center of Islamic Art and one of the most known artists the Middle East for this resourceful designs and inventive art. In 2005 he released "Muhammadeyat", a collection of 500 artwork designs generated from the word "Muhammad" in Arabic (please see below). The 500 designs are split into 11 groups (soft, square, hexagonal, octagonal, etc). Moreover, Mr. Al-Ali did a similar collection to "Muhammadeyat", but derived from the word "Allah".

Mohammed Mandi, Artist and Calligrapher, UAE

With his unique experience and creative designs, he was nominated to design the Arabic calligraphy on the banknotes and passports of UAE and many other countries. In addition, he was nominated to supervise calligraphic designs in Shaikh Zayed Grand Mosque in Abu Dhabi, UAE and many other mosques in the world.

An artistic design of the word "Muhammad" based on Arabic script (separate letters). It is the main component of the piece designed by Mr. Mandi which reflects transparent harmony between the artistic designs of the word "MUHAMMAD" in Arabic and English scripts.

Haji Noor Deen, Master Calligrapher, China

Born in 1963 in Shangdong province, China. He is one of the most renowned calligraphers who created a unique link between Chinese and Arabic calligraphy.

The artistic pieces indicate: "There is no God but Allah, Muhammad is the Messenger of Allah". The dome in the bottom part is formed from the statement "Muhammad is the Messenger of Allah"

Celina Cebula, Decorative Artist and Calligrapher, Poland

Graduated from Pedagogical University in Cracow and specialized in decorative art and artistic education. With her distinctive talent to mix calligraphy with painting she was able to reflect new meanings in her artistic designs.

The word Muhammad, the Messenger of God in Arabic mirrored over a colorful background

"Unless you show mercy to others, Allah will not be merciful to you".

"Who does not thank people does not thank God".

Muhammad Attributes Portrait by calligrapher A. Jaish

Award winning calligrapher Abdul Ilah Abu Jaish was honoured to carry out this attribute portrait in 2009.

"Hilya" is the Arabic name for the calligraphic art particularly related to the description of prophet Muhammad (pbuh). The calligraphic form of this "Hilya" is inspired by a mosque building shape with a recess containing the Arabic phrase "In the Name of God, Most Gracious, Most Merciful".

The portrait has a big circle as a mosque dome surrounded with four small circles as pillars under it and has an oblong representing the mosque open yard.

Calligraphers, throughout history, used to design calligraphic pieces using Arabic alphabets describing the attributes and features of Prophet Muhammad as an expression of their love to him.

Sheikh Zayed Grand Mosque, Abu Dhabi, UAE: *It is the largest mosque in the United Arab Emirates and the eighth largest mosque in the world. The mosque site is equivalent to the size of five football fields approximately. It can accommodate more than 40,000*

worshippers. It has 82 domes and 4 minarets each 107 m high. The mosque has the world's largest carpet which measures 5627 m^2 and the world's largest chandelier (15 m high and 10 m diameter). The mosque is considered as one of the most important tourist attractions in UAE.

Al-Saleh Mosque, Sanaa – Yemen: *It is the largest mosque in Yemen. It was opened in 2008, with an overall area of 224000 m2 approx. and a capacity of 40000 worshippers. The mosque was built in a Yemeni architectural style. It includes 15 wooden doors as well as 6 large minarets.*

Sultan Qaboos Grand Mosque, Oman: *It is the largest mosque in Oman. It was opened in 2001 and includes the world's second largest hand-woven carpet and chandelier. (mosque area - 416,000 sq. meters, complex of the mosque extends to 40,000 sq. meters).*

The Grand Mosque of Kuwait: *Photo taken by photographer Ahmed Al-Amiri on the 27th night of the holy month of fasting (Ramadan). The mosque accommodates more than 30000 worshippers*

Muslims fast the whole month of Ramadan from sunrise to sunset. At night, Muslims perform extra prayers and supplications.

The Museum of the Islamic Arts, Qatar: *Opened to the public in December 2008, designed by American architect I.M.Pei the famous designer of the Louvre in Pyramid. The displayed artifacts in the museum reflect the plurality and diversity in the arts of the Islamic world.*

233

The Jumeirah Mosque, Dubai, UAE: *One of the most attractive mosques in Dubai which reflects modern Islamic architecture.*

King Hussein Mosque, Amman, Jordan: *Was inaugurated in 2005 as one of the largest mosques in Amman that reflects the modern Islamic art and calligraphy. With its square shape and four minarets, it overlooks the city of Amman as it was built over a mount 1000 m approx above the sea level.*

Ahmed Al-Fateh Mosque, Kingdom of Bahrain: Was opened in 1988 by the late Amir of Bahrain, Sheikh Issa bin Salman Al-Khalifa. The mosque occupies an area of 6,500 square meters and it can accommodate up to 7000 worshippers. The mosque reflects a transparent blend of Islamic architecture and the local heritage.

Al-Aqsa Mosque, Jerusalem: It is believed by Muslims that it is the second mosque placed on the earth for humanity to worship one God (Note: the first one is the sacred mosque in Mecca). Al-Aqsa Mosque is a sacred place for Muslims and used to be the first Qiblah in Islam (the place Muslims used to direct their faces towards it when praying to God). After Quranic revelation from God, Muslims were commanded to change the "Qiblah" towards the Mosque of Sanctuary in Makkah which has the Kaaba (the cubical building built by Prophet Abraham (pbuh) to worship one God). The total area of Al-

Qibli Masjid

Aqsa Mosque/ Sanctuary is about 14.4 Hectare or 144000 m2. It includes two important shrines, the "Qibli Masjid" (where the Imam usually leads the prayers and the "Dome of the Rock".

Dome of the Rock – Jerusalem: *It is an Islamic shrine and a mosque built in the period of 688-692 CE by the Umayyad Caliph Abdul Malik Bin Marwan over the rock that is believed by Muslims the place where Prophet Muhammad (pbuh) ascended to the Heavens. It is an octagon building with a golden dome of 29.4m diameter.*

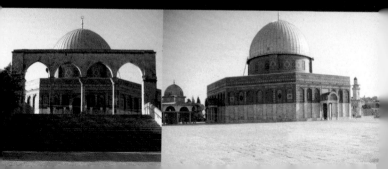

Umayyad Mosque, Damascus, Syria

The Ummayad Mosque, established (706 -715 CE) under the Umayyad caliph Al Walid. It is one of the largest and oldest mosques in the world that has a great architectural importance (mosque interior is approx 4000m².

The mosque holds a shrine which is believed to contain the head of St. John The Baptist (Prophet Yahya in Arabic), honored as a prophet by Muslims and Christians alike. In 2001 Pope John Paul II visited the mosque, primarily to visit the relics of John The Baptist. It was the first time a pope paid a visit to a mosque. The minaret in the southeast corner is called the Minaret of Jesus as many Muslims believe that when Jesus returns, he will descend near this Minaret.

The Great Mosque of Samarra, Iraq

It is a 9th century mosque which is located in the Iraqi city of Samarra. The mosque was commissioned in 848 and completed in 851 by the Abbasid Caliph Al-Mutawakkil.

The Great Mosque of Samarra was at one time the largest mosque in the world; its minaret, the Malwiya Tower, is a vast spiralling cone (snail shaped) 52 meters high and 33 meters wide with a spiral ramp. The mosque had 17 aisles, and its walls were panelled with mosaics of dark blue glass. Minaret is in the style of Babylonian ziggurat.

Sultan Ahmet Mosque - Turkey: *It is better known as the "Blue Mosque", with cascading domes and six slender minarets. Commissioned by Sultan Ahmet of the Ottoman Empire in the 17th century (Construction began in 1609 and took seven years).*

Ayasofya, Istanbul, Turkey :
*Aya Sofya (Hagia Sophia) in Istanbul – Turkey. It is a former Byzantine
church then served as an Ottoman mosque for approx 500 years. Now it is
a museum and a major tourist attraction place.*

Taj Mahal, Agra, India : This is not a mosque, but a mausoleum (burial building that reflects the Islamic Architechture) built by Shah Jahan (1592–1666) in memory of his wife. Due to its unique architectural design, it is considered as one of the most important tourist attractions in the world.

▲ *Jama Masjid in New Delhi, India* The largest mosque in India, built in 1656
▼ *Red Fort, Agra, India*

▲ Faisal Mosque, Islamabad, Pakistan   Lahore Fort in Pakistan ▼

▲ Star Mosque, Dhaka, Bangladesh   Auburn Gallipoli Mosque, Sydney, Australia ▼

▲ Sultan Mosque, Singapore   Sultan O. A. Saifuddin Mosque, Brunei ▼

▲ *Turkish Mosque in Tokyo, Japan*   *Mosque in Pattani, Thailand* ▼

▲ **The Crystal Mosque, Kuala Terengganu, Malaysia:**
The mosque is mainly made of Crystal. It is located at Islamic Heritage Park on the island of Wan Man. It was officially opened in 2008

Putrajaya Mosque, Malaysia ▼

▲ Kuantan Mosque in Malaysia   Mosque in Perak in Malaysia ▼

Al-Azhar Mosque in Cairo, Egypt: Established in 971 CE , connected

The Ahmad Ibn Tulun Mosque in Cairo, Egypt: Completed in 879 CE, one of the largest in the world, (26,318 sq m) it is also famed for its lovely architecture and unique minaret.

The Mezquita of Cordoba, Spain: *Mezquita is the Spanish word for "Mosque". It is an 8th Century Mosque designed by Islamic architects under the supervision of the Emir of Cordoba, Abdul-Rahman II (822-852). Today, the Mezquita is the Cathedral of Cordoba (officially the Cathedral of St. Mary of the Assumption).*

Alhambra Calat, Spain: Also called "the red fortress". It is a palace and fortress complex, constructed during the ruling of the Muslim Sultan of Granada (1353-1391 CE). Today it is one of Spain's major tourist attractions exhibiting the most famous Islamic architecture in Spain.

Note: Within Alhambra, the Palace of Roman Emperor Charles V was erected in 1527 CE.

The Hassan II Mosque, Casablanca, Morocco: *It was completed in 1993. Designed by French architect Michel Pinseau. The Great Mosque's minaret is the tallest structure in Morocco and the tallest minaret in the world (210 meters). At night, lasers shine a beam from the top of the minaret toward the Mosque of Sanctuary in Mecca. (Capacity: 25000 worshippers).*

The Kairaouine Mosque, Fes, Morocco: *Founded in 987 CE. It is the second largest mosque in Morocco (after the new Hassan II Mosque in Casablanca) and one of the oldest universities in the world. Also, it is the oldest Islamic monument in Fes.*

▲ Kipchak Mosque in Ashgabat Turkmenistan   Azadi Mosque in Ashgabat Turkmenistan ▼

▲ Shir Dor Madrasah - Samarkand, Uzbekistan   Mosque in Bukhara, Uzbekistan ▼

▲ *Kul Sharif Mosque in Kazan Russia*   *Mosque in Kazkhstan* ▼

▲ Mosque in USA

Stockholm mosque, Sweden ▼

The Grand Mosque of Paris, France: *It is the largest mosque in France. It was founded after World War I. Inaugurated on 15th July 1926.*

Note: In Islam there are five prayers a day. The following is a translation of the words of the "Azaan" (call for each prayer). Each statement is repeated twice: Allah is the Greatest. I bear witness that there is no deity but Allah. I bear witness that Muhammad is the Messenger of Allah. Come to the prayer. Come to the real success. Allah is the Greatest. There is no deity but Allah.

Mosque in Penzberg, Germany: The minaret is engraved with words of the "Azaan" the Muslim call for the daily prayers. The Arabic calligraphic design was made by award winner calligrapher Mohammed Mandi from UAE.

The Great Mosque of Xi'an, China

▲ *Grand Mosque in Indonesia*   *Hui Mosque in Ningxia, China* ▼

▲ *Great Mosque in Touba, Senegal*   *Mosque Faisal, Conakry, Guinea* ▼

▲ Mosque in Bobo Dioulasso Burkina Faso   Djenné Mosque in Mali ▼

Djenné is home to the world's largest mud mosque. This is more impressive than it may sound: the building is huge, and manages to be elegant both up close and from a distance. Two times a year all the city's residents drop everything, cart mud up from the nearby Bani river, and together they re-pack the Mosque walls.

References

Abdul Ghani, M. Ilyas, (2003). The History of Al-Madinah Al-Munawwarah, Rasheed Publishing, KSA

Ahmad, Mumtaz ,(1996). Islam and Democracy: The Emerging Consensus; Middle East Affairs Journal,

Al-Bouti, M.S.Ramadan, (2006). The Jurisprudence of Seerah (Muhammad's Life), Dar Al-Fikr, Damascus, Syria.

Al-Mutawa, Jassem, (2001). The Wives of the Prophet in Contemporary Time. Kuwait

Al-Mubarakpuri, Safi-ur-Rahman, (1996). The Sealed Nectar: Biography of the Noble Prophet Muhammad, Darussalam, KSA.

Armstrong, Karen, (2002). Islam: A Short History.

Armstrong, Karen, (1992). Muhammad: A Biography of the Prophet.

Armstrong, Karen, (2007). Muhammad: A Prophet for Our Time.

Al-Nawawi, Y.S., " Riyadh Al-Saliheen", 2003 Authentic Sayings of Prophet Muhammad, Arabic Cover –Cairo –Egypt

As-Sallaabee, Ali Muhammad , "The noble life of the Prophet" , Darussalam, KSA

Bukhari, Mohammad Bin Ismael (Imam Abu Abdullah), (1997). Saheeh Bukhari, International Ideas Home – Amman –Jordan

Cleary, Thomas, (2001). The Wisdom of the Prophet: The Sayings of Muhammad

Gulen, M. Fethullah, (2000). Prophet Muhammad: Aspects of His Life, The Fountain, Viginia, USA.

Hammad, Ahmad Zaki (2007), The Gracious Qur'an: A Modern-Phrased Interpretation in English, Lucent Interpretations, IL, USA

Hart, Michael, (1992), "The 100; A Ranking of the Most Influential Persons in History":,1992, Carol Publishing Group. N.J. –USA

Islam, Yusuf, (1995). "The Life of the Last Prophet", Darussalam, Saudi Arabia

Khalidi, Tarif (2009). Images of Muhammad: Narratives of the Prophet in Islam Across the Centuries. Kindle Edition

Khan, M. Muhsin, " Sahih Al-Bukhari –English Translation", 4th Ed, 1985, Beirut- Lebanon

Montgomery Watt, W.(1974). Muhammad: Prophet and Statesman. Kindle Edition

Pickthall, Marmaduke (2006). The Qur'an Translated: Message for Humanity – The International Committee for the Support of the Final Prophet, Washington- USA

Ramadan, Tariq; (2009) In the Footsteps of the Prophet: Lessons from the Life of Muhammad

Saheeh Int. (2004), The Qur'an English Meanings. Abul-Qassim Publishing –Al Muntada Al-Islami-Jeddah- KSA

Sultan Sohaib N., Ali, Yusuf Ali, and Smith, Jane I. (2007), The Qur'an and Sayings of Prophet Muhammad: Selections Annotated & Explained (Skylight Illuminations)

Unal, Ali., "The Holy Qur'an With Annotated Interpretation in Modern English", 2006 , The Light –New Jersey, USA

Wolfe, Michael & Kronemer, Alex (2002). Muhammad: Legacy of a Prophet (DVD - Dec 18, 2002)

Yusuf, Hamza, (2003) The Life of the Prophet Muhammad (24 Audio CDs).

NOTES

For feedback, comments and enquiries, please write to
info@muhammadpocketguide.com